The Ordnance Survey
Map Skills Book

CHRIS WARN

ARNOLD-WHEATON

This book is jointly published by Arnold-Wheaton and Ordnance Survey.

Contents

Acknowledgements

The maps in this publication are reproduced from Ordnance Survey maps with the permission of the Controller of H.M.S.O.

Illustrated by Oxford Illustrators Ltd

Photographs by Chris Warn

Cover photograph by Studio 4, Exeter

The author and publisher thank the following for the use of additional material:

Aerofilms Ltd

Bristol Omnibus Company Ltd

Glenrothes Development Corporation

Merseyside Passenger Transport Executive

Have you ever climbed to the top of a high building and looked straight down to the streets below? At first it's very frightening, but you soon begin to enjoy looking at the world from this new angle.

We usually see the world from a *horizontal viewpoint*. A map, on the other hand, shows things in **plan view,** from a *vertical viewpoint*. This means that it shows the landscape from above, as you would see it from an aeroplane or a high building.

Imagine you are going for a ride in a helicopter. As the helicopter takes off, you can see the whole of the field you were standing in, the people waving to you, and all the trees around the edges. As the helicopter climbs, the field seems to become smaller and smaller. The higher you go, the more you can see, but in less and less detail. The people soon look like specks and the trees are just a green fuzz. Eventually, you have trouble picking out exactly which field you took off from, although you can see motorways, rivers and railways as lines stretching far into the distance.

Some maps show small areas in detail. Others show large areas in outline. This is what we mean by **scale.**

If you were in a helicopter or at the top of a high building you could easily see the relationship between one landmark and another; you could see how far apart they were and, if you had a compass, you could find the **direction** to go in to get from one to the other. Maps save you the trouble of climbing a high building and the expense of a helicopter ride!

So maps show things in **plan view,** they show the landscape **to scale** and they show the **direction** in which to go.

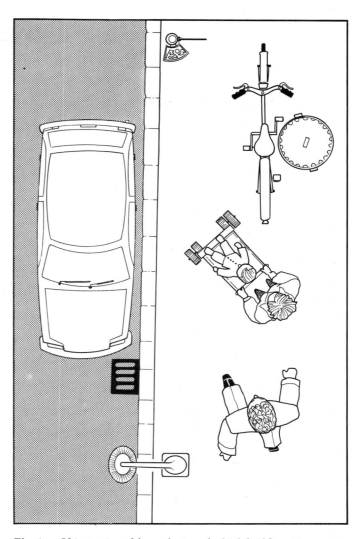

Fig. 1   *Objects viewed from the top of a high building. Can you guess what they are?*

Photo 1

Exercise 1
1. *Sketch the following things in plan view: a flag-pole, a church with a steeple, a lighthouse, a windmill.*
2. *At home, try to sketch a plan view of your house. Remember, you will not be able to see doors or windows!*
3. *Read the paragraph about the helicopter ride again. Sketch what you might see in the field from which the helicopter took off*
   (a) *when you had just lifted off,*
   (b) *when you were hovering at a height of about 500 metres above the ground,*
   (c) *when you were much higher up, hovering at a height of 1000 metres above the ground.*

Exercise 2
What famous building in London is shown here in plan view in a vertical air photograph? What does the building look like at street-level?

Answer: St Paul's Cathedral

1:50 000 Second Series Map
CONVENTIONAL SIGNS

Ordnance Survey

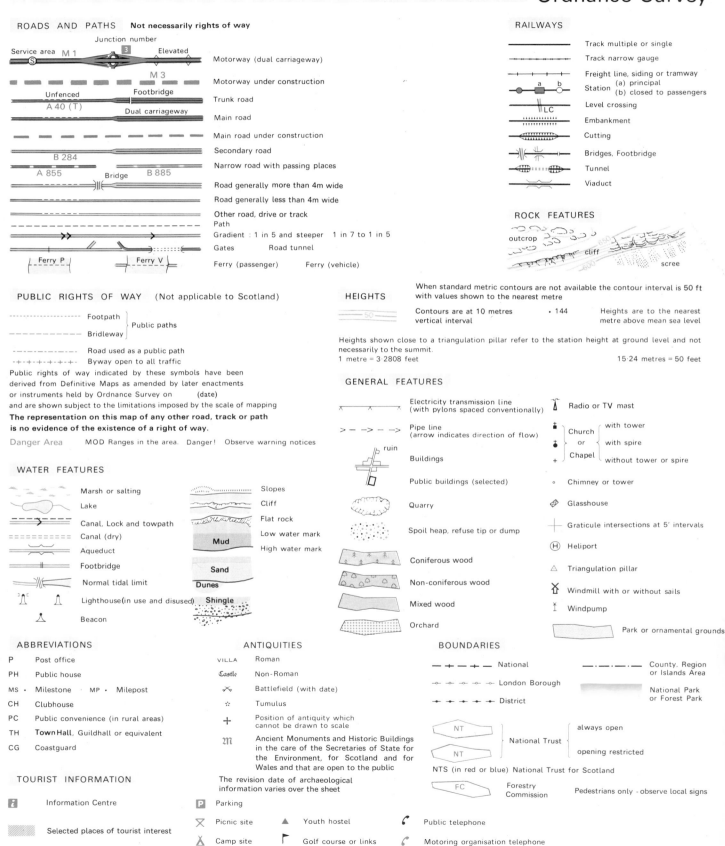

Imagine trying to print plan-view pictures of every building in a square kilometre on a piece of paper 20 mm square. That's what the Ordnance Survey have to do with their most popular type of map, the Landranger Series. The scale of Landranger maps is 1:50 000 (one to fifty thousand).

Obviously, some simple symbols that everyone will understand are needed, to show buildings, roads, woodland and so on. The symbols on Ordnance Survey maps are known as *conventional signs* ('conventional' because they are used by convention, or agreement, by everyone). On the opposite page you will see the conventional signs used on OS (Ordnance Survey) Landranger maps. Compare the drawings of a windmill, a lighthouse and a church with a steeple you did for Exercise 1 with the OS symbols. Which are easier to understand, your sketches or their symbols?

Exercise 3

1. *The sketch-map (Fig. 3) shows an imaginary landscape near a motorway in a country district. Make your own copy of this map, but instead of labelling different features in words, for example: 'Post Office' or 'Quarry', use the correct conventional signs. Colour your map with the correct colours.*

2. *Draw a sketch-map of the village described below, using only the correct conventional signs (as no directions are given, everyone's map will be different):*

   'Bridgeworth is a small village near to where the A51 trunk-road (dual carriageway) crosses the B5173. In the centre of the village, which is 1 km from the trunk-road, there is a chapel, a public house, an old castle owned by the National Trust, a youth hostel and a picnic site. On the other side of the trunk-road, the landscape is not so pleasant, for there are two electricity transmission lines, an old refuse-tip and a quarry served by a freight railway line.'

3. *Find out what the following words mean: multiple track, embankment, viaduct, aqueduct, Guild-hall, coniferous wood, ornamental grounds.*

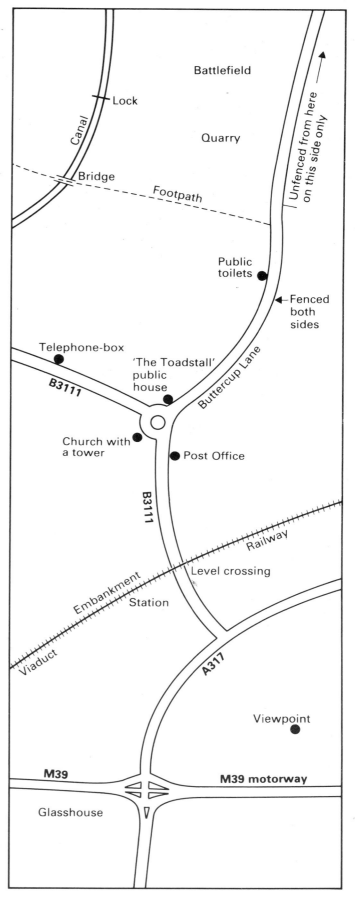

Fig. 2 *Symbols used on OS 1:50 000 scale maps*

Fig. 3

Fig. 4.1

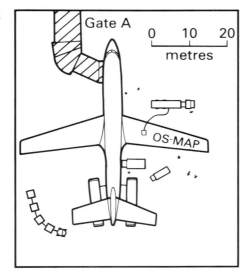

Fig. 4.2

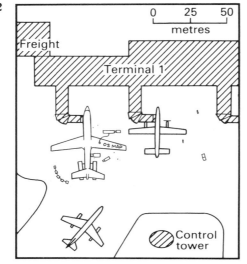

Fig. 4.3

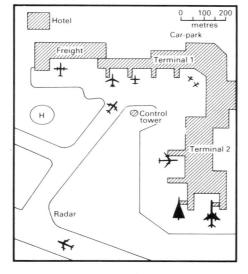

Figures 4.1, 4.2 and 4.3 are plan views of the same airport, drawn to different scales. The first one is the **largest-scale** plan; we can see the aeroplane at Gate A in Terminal 1 in quite a lot of detail. (How many different sorts of vehicles can you identify?) The third plan shows much more of the layout of the whole terminal area, although it tells us very little about Gate A; it is a **smaller-scale** plan.

Try drawing a fourth plan, to show the whole airport, including the runways and approach-roads. Your map will be a small-scale one, showing a large area in very little detail; each building will be tiny. (Notice that large-scale maps are usually called *plans*, while smaller-scale maps are called *maps*.)

The aeroplane labelled OS-MAP in Fig. 4.1 really measures 50 metres from one wing-tip to the other. The same distance is only 50 mm on our plan, which means that our plan makes the aircraft look a thousand times smaller than it really is. This scale reduction could be recorded in three ways:

1. *In words.* For example, '50 mm represents 50 metres', or '1 mm represents 1 metre'.
2. *By drawing a scale line,* as we have done in the top right-hand corner of the plans of the airport.
3. *By using a representative fraction.* For example, if 1 mm represents 1 metre, and there are 1000 mm in 1 metre, the representative fraction is 1:1000 (one to one thousand). The standard Ordnance Survey map scale of 1:50 000 means that for every 1 mm on the map there are 50 000 mm on the ground. The scale of Fig. 4.1 is 1:1000, so the objects drawn in the plan are one thousand times smaller than the real thing.

Ordnance Survey maps range from detailed **large-scale plans** of streets to **small-scale maps** showing the whole of Britain.

Exercise 4

1. *The four maps on page 7 each show the Isle of Wight at different scales. Which is best for seeing*
   (a) *a view of the whole island?*
   (b) *the position of the island within the British Isles?*
   (c) *the roads around Yarmouth?*
   (d) *the distances from the island to London and Bristol?*
2. *What additional information about Yarmouth appears on Map 2 that is not shown on Map 1?*
3. *Use the most suitable map to answer these questions.*
   (a) *How far is it from Lymington to Yarmouth by ferry?*
   (b) *How long does this ferry journey take?*
   (c) *At what speed does the ferry travel?*

SCALE 1:50 000

Fig. 5   *Scale line from an OS 1:50 000 scale map*

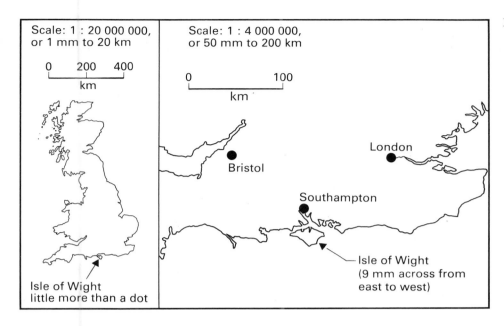

Fig. 6

Scale: 1 : 20 000 000, or 1 mm to 20 km

Isle of Wight little more than a dot

Scale: 1 : 4 000 000, or 50 mm to 200 km

Bristol

London

Southampton

Isle of Wight (9 mm across from east to west)

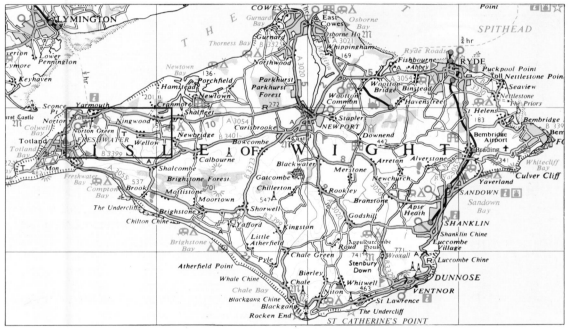

Map 1

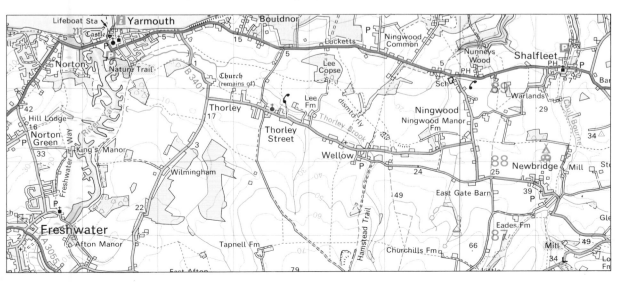

Map 2

GRID REFERENCES

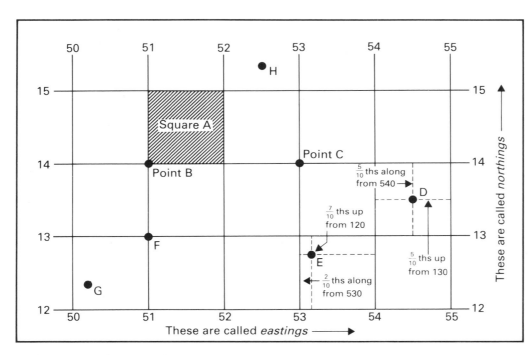

Fig. 7 *These grid squares are drawn to the scale of 1:50 000. Each square measures 20 mm x 20 mm and represents a 1-kilometre square on the ground.*
Square A is given the four-figure reference 5114.
Point B is given the six-figure reference 510140.
Point C is at 530140, Point D at 545135 and Point E at 532127.
What are the grid references for Points F, G and H?

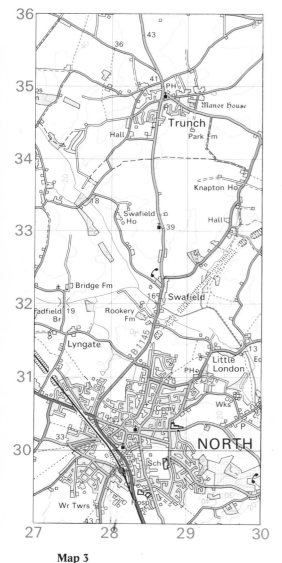

Map 3

The lines drawn across Ordnance Survey maps, forming a 'net' of squares, are called **grid lines.** You can see them on Map 3. The distance between grid lines represents 1 kilometre, so each square on the map represents a square kilometre on the ground.

Each grid line is numbered. The lines running from north to south are called **eastings,** because their numbers increase eastwards. The others run from west to east and are called **northings,** because their numbers increase northwards.

We use eastings and northings to refer to either a whole square or a specific point on the map. Always read the eastings first, then the northings.

To give a grid reference for a square, give the numbers of the grid lines that cross at the bottom left-hand (south-west) corner of the square. Give the number of the easting first, then the northing. The grid reference for square A, for example, is easting 51, northing 14, or, put together, 5114. This is a *four-figure reference.*

To refer to a specific point, use a *six-figure reference.* To say how many tenths of a square that point is between one grid line and the next, add a number between zero and nine to each grid line number. Point B, for example, is at easting 51 and zero tenths and northing 14 and zero tenths, or 510140. Point D is at easting 54 and five tenths and northing 13 and five tenths, or 545135. Try a few and you'll soon get the hang of it.

Remember, **eastings first, northings second,** or 'along the corridor, then up the stairs'.

Exercise 5
1. *What would you find at 286331, 282297, 287322 and 297303 on Map 3?*
2. *Name the farm in square 2732.*
3. *Give a four-figure reference for the square containing Knapton House.*
4. *Give six-figure references for the public house in Little London, the cemetery and the hospital in the town (North Walsham) and the Hall in the south-west of Trunch village.*

Right at the beginning we said that maps show things in plan view, show things to scale, and show us direction. Directions can be given either as *points of the compass* (for example, north-east, south-south-west) or as *compass bearings*, which are measured in degrees (0° to 360°), going clockwise from north. East is 90°, south is 180°, south-west is 225°, and so on. Can you label the unmarked points of the compass and compass bearings in Fig. 8.1 and Fig. 8.2?

It is not as simple as you might imagine to define the word 'north'. The direct line from any place to the North Pole is called **true north.** If you follow a magnetic compass northwards, you will reach not the North Pole but the earth's magnetic pole, which is in Arctic Canada and is constantly moving. This is called **magnetic north.** Finally, there is **grid north.** The grid lines on a map seldom point exactly to true north, because the earth is spherical and a map is flat. Lines of longitude drawn on a globe or a world map all meet at the North Pole, so they taper gradually towards each other. Grid lines, on the other hand, stay the same distance apart, because they are parallel to each other. If you follow the grid lines on a map northwards, you will be following grid north.

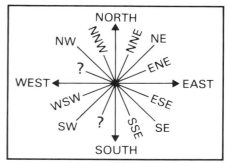

Fig. 8.1   *Points of the compass*

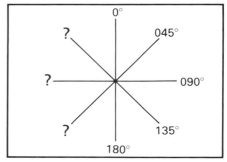

Fig. 8.2   *Compass bearings*

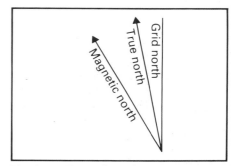

Fig. 8.3   *Types of 'north'*

Exercise 6

Look again at Map 3 (opposite). Give all directions with reference to grid north. Find the railway station at 283297. The railway line runs generally from NW to SE. More exactly, it goes southwards on a bearing of 160° and northwards on a bearing of 323°.

1. *In which direction does the disused railway near Swafield run?*
2. *What is the bearing of Rookery Farm from Bridge Farm?*
3. *What landmarks are 500 metres south-west of the railway station?*
4. *Look at Fig. 9. A ship has to sail from seaport A and call at seaports B, C and D before returning to A. Give compass directions to the captain to steer him safely to each seaport.*
5. *An airliner has to fly from airport X to Y, and then to Z. It must not fly over the Danger zone. Plot the route and give the pilot bearings for each leg.*

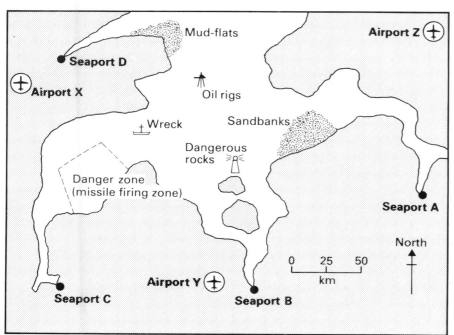

Fig. 9

HEIGHT AND SLOPES

Imagine a reservoir that is gradually drained of water during a summer drought. Every time the water-level drops, a new shoreline is created. Lines showing the position of former shorelines may be seen running round the sides of the reservoir. The diagrams show this happening.

Photo 2 (below) shows the San Juan River in the western U.S.A. cutting through over a thousand metres of horizontally bedded rock. The rock outcrops, or layers, can clearly be seen on the steep sides of the canyon.

Both these examples show the lines made by horizontal planes meeting a hillslope. They also illustrate what we mean by **contour lines.**

Contour lines on maps are lines joining places of equal height. The 40-, 50-, 60- and 70-metre shorelines in the drawings of the reservoir are contour lines. So are the rock outcrops on the sides of the canyon in the photograph. The brown contour lines on OS maps are drawn in by the map-makers; you cannot see them on the ground.

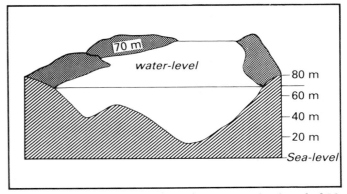

Fig. 10.1 *When this reservoir was full its water-level reached 70 metres above sea-level. During an exceptionally dry summer, the water-level began to drop.*

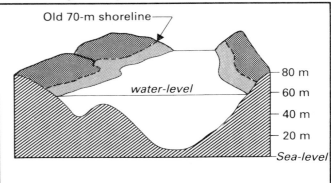

Fig. 10.2 *By 1 June the level had fallen to 60 metres above sea-level.*

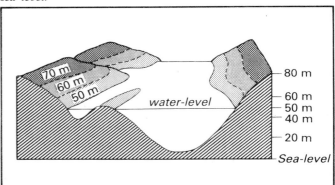

Fig. 10.3 *By 1 July no rain had fallen, and the level was down to 50 metres. An island appeared.*

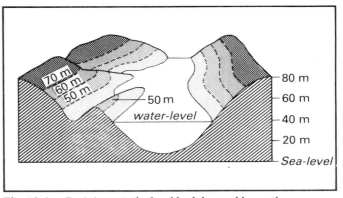

Fig. 10.4 *By 1 August, the level had dropped lower than ever: just 40 metres above sea-level. Trace this drawing and work out what the reservoir looked like on 1 September, when the water-level had fallen a further 10 metres.*

Photo 2 *The San Juan River, Utah, has cut a deep canyon through many layers of rock.*

The intervals between contour lines may represent any height difference the map-maker chooses. The reservoir sides, for example, had contours at 10-metre *vertical intervals* (at a *vertical separation* of 10 metres). OS Landranger maps also use the 10-metre contour interval.

One rule that will soon become clear is: **the closer the contour lines, the steeper the slope.**

TYPES OF SLOPES

Photo 3

An **even slope** has the same rate of rise (called the *gradient*) throughout its length. Contours are evenly spaced.

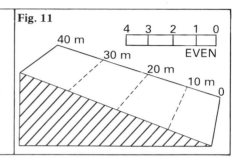

Fig. 11

Photo 4

A **convex slope** has a steep gradient at the bottom and a shallow gradient at the top. Contours are closer together at the bottom.

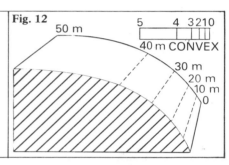

Fig. 12

Photo 5

A **concave slope** has a shallow gradient at the bottom and a steep gradient at the top. Contours are closer together at the top.

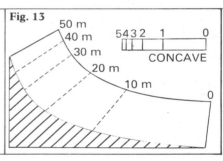

Fig. 13

Photo 6

A **compound slope** has several variations of gradient from top to bottom. Contours may be bunched together at several points up the hillslope.

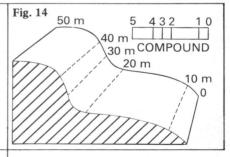

Fig. 14

Photo 7

A **cliff** is a vertical (or very steep) rock-face. Maps tend to use a black symbol (see page 4) rather than contours.

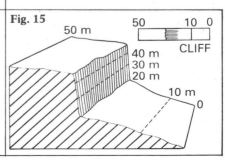

Fig. 15

Now that we know that contour lines show us both the height of land and the shape of slopes, we can look at different contour patterns to see how landscape features are represented on OS maps.

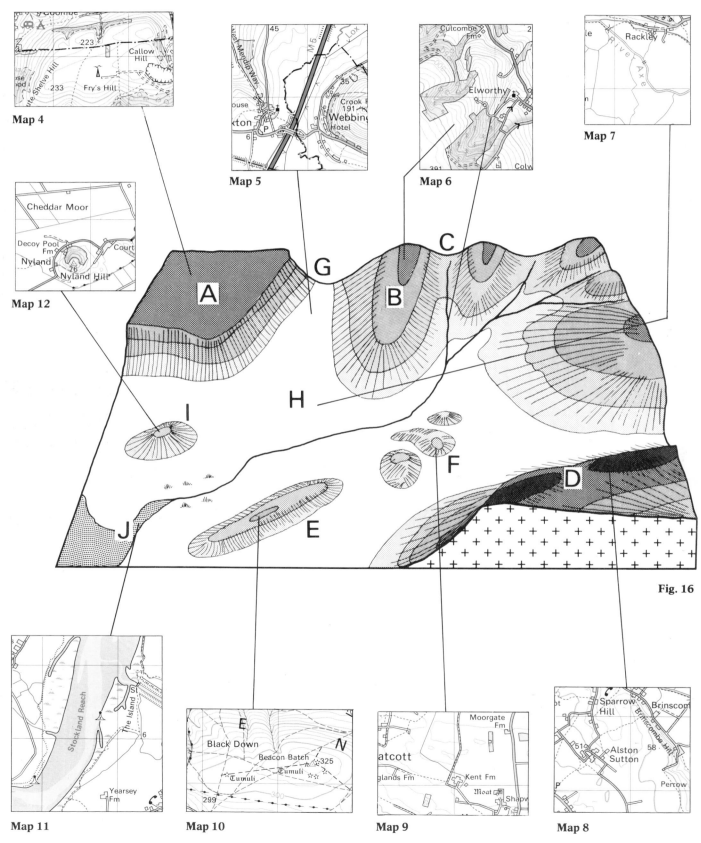

Map 4

Map 5

Map 6

Map 7

Map 12

Fig. 16

Map 11

Map 10

Map 9

Map 8

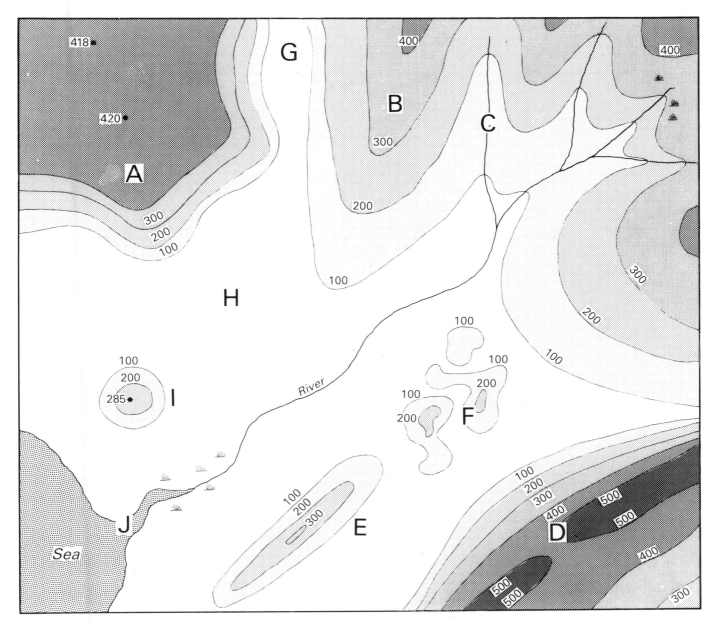

Fig. 17 *Which letters (A to J) refer to which features?*

NAME	DESCRIPTION	LETTER
Knoll	Isolated hill	I
Plateau	Flat-topped hill	A
Ridge	Long, thin, 'sausage-shaped' hill	E
Spur	Finger of high land pointing into low land	B
Escarpment	Hill with one steep side (*scarp slope*) and one gently sloping side (*dip slope*)	D
Undulating land	Low, hummocky land, going gently up and down	F
Valley	Low land with higher land on either side; contours shaped like arrowheads pointing upstream	G
Gap or Pass	Low route between two hills	
Estuary	Tidal section of a river valley	J
Plain	Low, flat land	H

Map 13

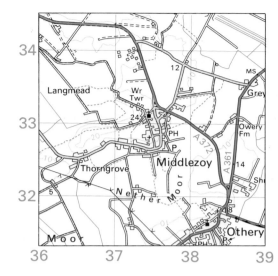

Contour lines are not the only way of representing height above sea-level on a map. If you look at Map 13 you will see spots with numbers beside them scattered about. These are **spot heights.** Except for a small ridge which rises to 24 metres above sea-level, the area shown on the map is very low-lying, with spot heights ranging from 5 to 14 metres. It is a very suitable place for an airfield. Without the spot heights there would be very little information about the relief of the Middlezoy area, where there are only a few contour lines.

Surveyors use the *bench mark* on triangulation pillars to measure the height of other places above sea-level. The heights of these pillars, which appear on OS maps as a blue spot inside a triangle, are *carefully measured.* To calculate the height of another place, a surveyor measures its distance from a triangulation pillar and the angle up or down from the pillar.

Map-makers start with a mass of spot heights, then draw the contours in around them.

Photo 8
A triangulation pillar

Exercise 7
Make a tracing of the map below. Join up the spot heights with contour lines at 50-metre vertical intervals. Part of the 150-metre contour line has been drawn in as an example. Remember that contour lines never cross each other, and are usually smooth in shape. Heights other than 50, 100, 150, 200, 250 and 300 metres are there to help you.

If you complete this task successfully you will have a landscape with several river valleys. Can you draw in where the rivers will flow?

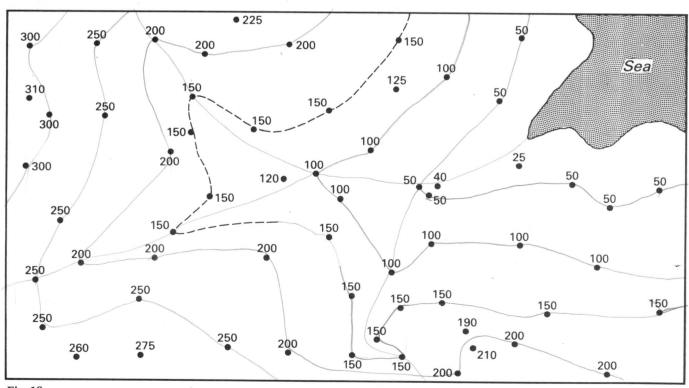

Fig. 18

Photo 9   *The Bowmont Valley, Northumberland*

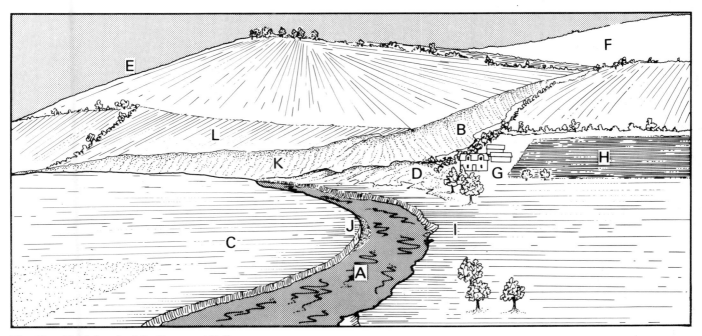

Fig. 19   *Field sketch of the Bowmont Valley*

Exercise 8

This is a chance to test some of the ideas covered so far on an example of the beautiful scenery to be found in the Cheviot Hills.

1. *Contrast rivers A and B in Fig. 19. How would they differ on an OS Map?*
2. *How does the lowland at C and D differ? Would contours show this?*
3. *What type of slope is found at E? How will it appear on a map?*
4. *Why is there snow on hill F but not hill E?*
5. *Why do you think the farmer chose to build his farm-house at G?*
6. *Why do you think that field H is the only one suitable for ploughing?*
7. *Why do you think the river bank is wearing away and collapsing at I, but opposite at J there is silt being added to the side of the river channel? What is a bend in a river called?*
8. *Why is the land at K left in a rough state whilst the land at L has been improved to give grazing land?*

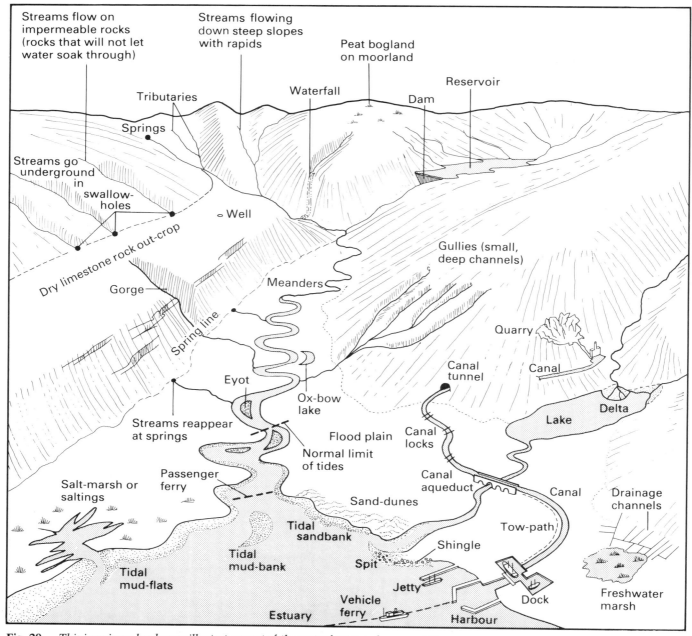

Streams flow on impermeable rocks (rocks that will not let water soak through)

Streams flowing down steep slopes with rapids

Peat bogland on moorland

Reservoir

Tributaries

Waterfall

Dam

Springs

Streams go underground in swallow-holes

Well

Gullies (small, deep channels)

Dry limestone rock out-crop

Gorge

Meanders

Spring line

Quarry

Canal tunnel

Canal

Eyot

Ox-bow lake

Lake

Delta

Streams reappear at springs

Flood plain

Canal locks

Normal limit of tides

Canal aqueduct

Canal

Drainage channels

Salt-marsh or saltings

Passenger ferry

Sand-dunes

Tow-path

Tidal sandbank

Shingle

Tidal mud-bank

Spit

Freshwater marsh

Tidal mud-flats

Jetty

Dock

Vehicle ferry

Estuary

Harbour

Fig. 20   *This imaginary landscape illustrates most of the water features shown on OS maps.*

Rivers usually begin from *springs* or *bogland* near the summits of hills and moorland. They may start flowing in deep, narrow channels called *gullies*. Soon they will join other *tributaries* to form *streams*. Generally these streams descend in *torrents* or rough, white water over *waterfalls* and *rapids*.

When these streams reach lower land, they widen into rivers and flow over a *flood plain*. Usually this gets wider towards the mouth of the river. The river will wind in a series of *meanders*. Some of these will be bypassed to leave *ox-bow lakes*. Near the sea, the river may split into silty islands called *eyots*. Most rivers enter the sea in tidal *estuaries*. Sand, shingle, mud or silt will be exposed along the estuary sides when the tide goes down.

Some rocks are *impermeable*, which means that they will not allow rainwater to soak through (like the roof of a house). Others, such as chalk and limestone, are *permeable*, and soak up surface-water. Streams going from impermeable to permeable rocks often disappear underground in *swallow-holes*, later to re-emerge as *springs* at the base of the permeable rock outcrop. Underground in limestone areas are caves and caverns. Sometimes these collapse to form a *gorge*.

We influence water features in many ways. We can store water in *reservoirs*, move it through *pipelines* and dispose of it with *drainage schemes*. We can straighten and dredge rivers, and build *canals* with such features as locks, tow-paths and aqueducts.

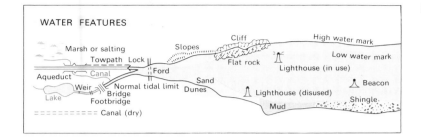

Fig. 21 *OS symbols for water features*

Photo 10 *Aerial view of Alnmouth, Northumberland*

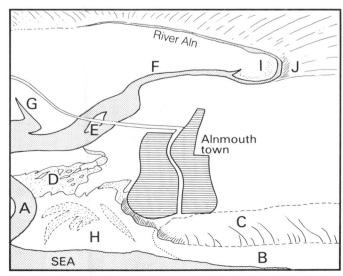

Fig. 22

Exercise 9

The photograph and the field sketch show the mouth of the River Aln as it joins the North Sea at Alnmouth in Northumberland.

1. *Using information on this page and the facing page, try to work out which of the following features correspond to the letters A to J:*
   sand-dunes, flood plain, tidal estuary, eyot, salting, drained land, deposition on inside of a meander bend, river cliff on the outside of a meander bend, sandy beach, tidal mud-flats.
2. *Bearing in mind that this photograph was taken at low tide, try to work out where the high-water mark would be. At what point up the River Aln is the normal tidal limit?*
3. *Try to draw a map of the estuary using the correct conventional signs for water features.*

VILLAGE SITES

Most villages were established several centuries ago. Many are over 700 years old. We have to try to imagine the land as the original settlers saw it, a natural landscape with far more trees and marshy areas than there are today. We also have to remember that they had no piped water, modern earth-moving equipment or modern defence-systems. This meant that access to good-quality farming land, freedom from flooding, access to drinking-water, and a site that could be defended against raiding-parties were all important considerations. Some villages grew up where several routes converged, perhaps at the lowest bridging-point of an estuary, or at the foot of a mountain pass.

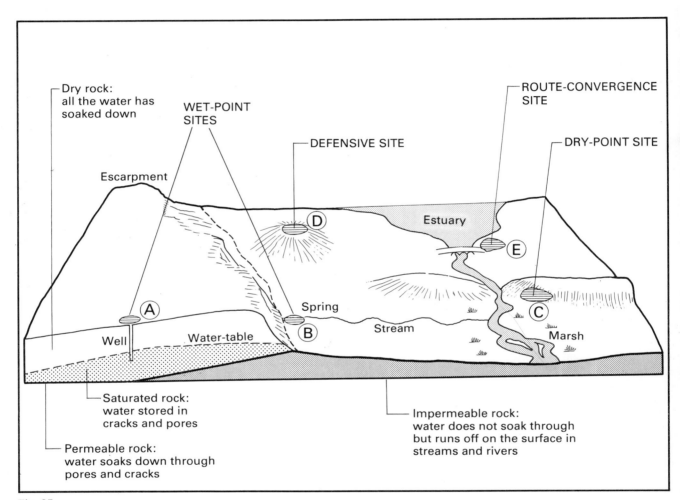

Fig. 23

Sites A and B These are both examples of **wet-point sites.** That means that they are located at a reliable source of water in an otherwise dry area. (The diagram suggests why the hills between A and B have very few surface streams and rivers.) Village A is clustered round a *well,* which is sunk to a depth that will reach the *water-table* (the level below which the joints and pores in the rock are filled with water).

Village B is located along a *spring line* at the junction between the outcrops of the permeable and impermeable rock. Here water emerges from the pores and joints of the permeable rock to flow on top of the impermeable rock as a stream. Spring-line villages are common at such locations as the foot of the escarpments (see page 13) of the chalk hills of Southern England (for example, the Chilterns and the North and South Downs), the oolitic limestone hills of the South and East Midlands (for example, the Cotswolds and Lincoln Edge) and the carboniferous limestone rocks of the Pennines.

The four villages shown in the 1:50 000 scale OS maps are Whitwell on the Isle of Wight; Lyndhurst in the New Forest (Hampshire); Kinnaird in Fife and Clewer in Somerset.

Which one occupies

(a) *a wet-point site?* (c) *a defensive site?*
(b) *a dry-point site?* (d) *a route-convergence site?*

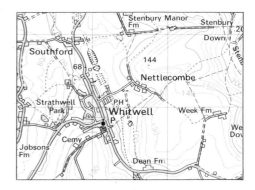

Map 14

Site C This is an example of a **dry-point site.** The village is located on a low hill above a marshy area. Before the days of modern flood- and drainage-control, it would have been too dangerous to live on the marshland. This site gave farmers access to the high-quality pasture land on the edge of the marsh-lands during dry weather as well as a safe retreat from flooding after severe storms. Such dry-point sites were very common in East Anglia and the Fens where low clay hills provided natural flood-protection. Sometimes villagers built their own mounds. Another very common dry-point site was a river terrace, a flat area of gravel or silt above flood-level. Even the City of London began on such a site.

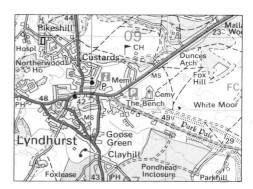

Map 15

Site D In prehistoric times, and from the end of the Roman occupation until about 1600, local **defence** was of great concern to villagers and townsfolk alike. Raiding-parties would try to steal their cattle, crops and valuable possessions. Ease of defence was there-fore an important consideration when the location of a village was chosen. It was hard for men armed with arrows and spears to attack a village set on a spur or an isolated hill (see page 13), so a location like Site D was a good, safe one.

Map 16

Site E Often villages and towns grew up at a **route convergence.** This might be, as shown here, at the lowest bridging-point of a river. Further downstream, the only way to cross the river was by boat. People living along the banks of the estuary would need to travel through E in order to cross the bridge. Inns and shops would develop here, providing jobs for settlers. Other convergence-points include the foot of a mountain pass and the junction of two major roads.

Map 17

VILLAGE SHAPES

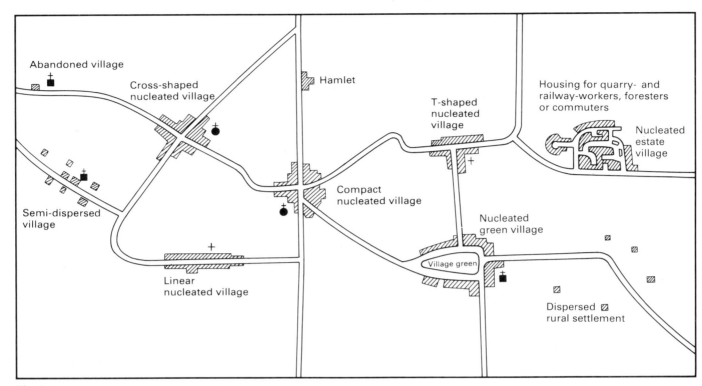

Fig. 24

Many established villages have very clearly defined shapes when seen on a map or from the air. Sometimes, as in the case of Warkworth (shown in the photograph) that shape is largely the result of the site that it occupies. Some villages

1. are strung out along a main road;
2. are closely packed together around the centre;
3. grow along each arm of a crossroads;
4. cluster around a village green, an open space that was often used to protect cattle from raiders at night;
5. were built as a housing estate for rural workers or commuters;
6. grow along the three arms of a road junction.

Using the sketch-map above, find the correct technical names for descriptions 1 to 6.

Not everyone who lives in a country area lives in a village. Some people live in scattered, or *dispersed*, farms or in a small cluster of houses called a *hamlet*.

In the Middle Ages most farm-workers lived in villages, often some distance from the fields they cultivated. When the enclosure regulations were brought in at the end of the eighteenth century many people moved out of villages into farmhouses nearer their fields. Left empty, some of the houses in the villages became derelict and fell down, leaving gaps like missing teeth. Such villages are known as *semi-dispersed* villages.

Some villages have been completely abandoned, except perhaps for the old parish church, which now stands by itself.

Photo 11   *Aerial view of Warkworth, Northumberland*

Exercise 11
Warkworth lies just inland from Alnmouth (see page 17) on the River Coquet.
1. *What can you say about its site? Draw a simple sketch-map with appropriate labels to make your answer clearer.*
2. *What can you say about the shape of the village? How is its shape affected by the river, the castle and the bridge?*
3. *Comment on the location of the buildings outside the village core.*

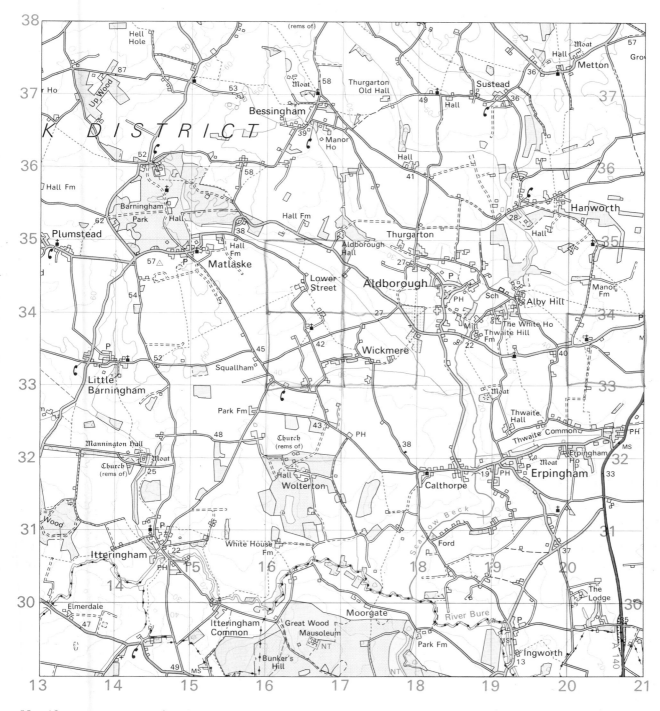

Map 18

Exercise 12

Map 18 shows part of Norfolk, which for many centuries has been a prosperous farming district. Until the start of the nineteenth century most people lived in nucleated villages, but since then there has been a trend towards the partial dispersion of homes outside the villages.

1. *Which of these squares has the most dispersed settlement: 1734, 1633, 1634, 2033?*

2. *Look at the shapes of the following villages on Map 18*

and choose the name on Fig. 24 that best fits each one: (a) Wickmere, (b) Aldborough, (c) Matlaske, (d) Itteringham, (e) Plumstead.

3. *Find an example of a hamlet and a seemingly abandoned village.*

4. *Which villages seem to be attached to large halls or manor-houses? Why was this once common?*

5. *Are new housing estates attached to any of the villages?*

SERVICES IN VILLAGES AND COUNTRY TOWNS

There are some items of shopping that you are likely to need every few days, like vegetables, bread or newspapers. Other more specialized items, such as cameras, furniture or shoes, are likely to be bought only occasionally. When you do buy these items, it is usually worth travelling to a big town or city where there is a wide choice at discount prices. Generally speaking, the more expensive or the more specialized an item is, the further you would be prepared to travel to buy it.

Small settlements have only very simple services, like a pub or a general store, while market towns have specialist services, like hospitals, solicitors, technical colleges and jewellery shops. Maps can help us spot the range of services that a settlement offers, although they do not indicate the types of shops.

A **hamlet** has only a few houses clustered together. It will probably have no services at all, except perhaps for a very tiny general store in one of the houses.

Photo 12   *A Scottish hamlet*

A **village** will have a few shops selling non-specific *consumable* items such as groceries, meat, newspapers, sweets and simple medicines. If it is an attractive village it may have a gift shop, a guest -house and a café. It may have a primary school.

Photo 13   *A village in Suffolk*

A **sub-town** is half-way between a village and a town in size. It may have such services as a bank, a police station, a doctor and a dentist.

Photo 14   *Welshpool, Powys, a sub-town*

A **market town** has not only a market, but secondary schools, a wide range of shops, several banks, a hospital and a bus station. Many shops sell *durable* items, such as electrical goods and furniture.

Photo 15   *The market town of Spalding, Lincolnshire*

Exercise 13

1. *Copy and complete this chart, which refers to the area around Aylsham in Norfolk (Map 19).*

Services shown on the map (tick if present)	church	post office	public house	public telephone	school	cemetery	mill	goods yard on railway	hospital	Is it a hamlet, village, sub-town or market town?
Oulton Street										
Cawston										
Marsham										
Blickling										
The Grange										
Aylsham										

2. *What information (in addition to that available on Map 19) would help you get a better idea of the services present in these settlements?*

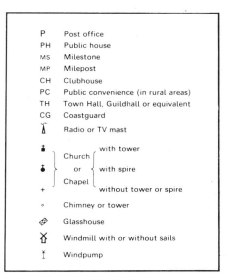

P	Post office
PH	Public house
MS	Milestone
MP	Milepost
CH	Clubhouse
PC	Public convenience (in rural areas)
TH	Town Hall, Guildhall or equivalent
CG	Coastguard

Radio or TV mast

Church with tower

or with spire

Chapel without tower or spire

○ Chimney or tower

Glasshouse

Windmill with or without sails

Windpump

Fig. 25 *Some of the symbols used on OS 1 : 50 000 maps*

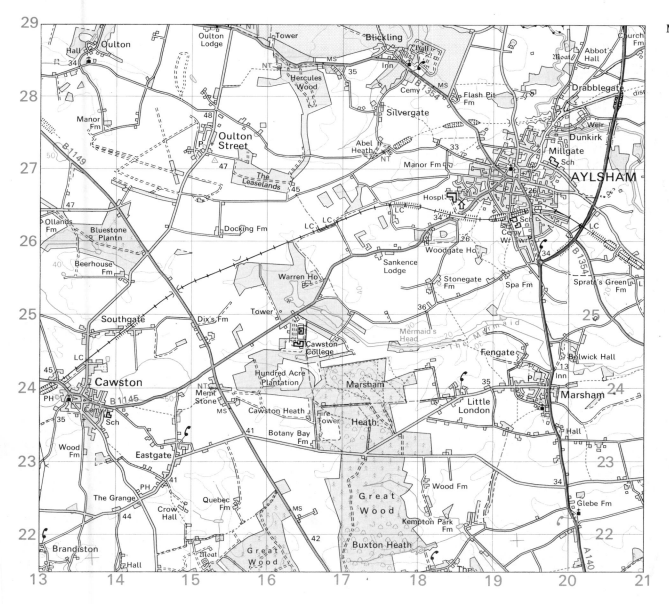

Map 19

Phase 1 *Roman towns*
These were compact, walled settlements with a well-planned layout, built between the first and the fifth centuries.

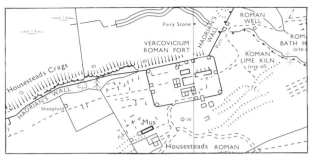
Map 20

Photo 16

Phase 2 *Medieval towns*
These were crowded, un-planned settlements enclosed by walls, generally built between the twelfth and sixteenth centuries.

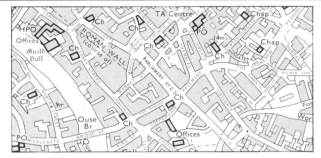
Map 21

Photo 17

Phase 3 *Georgian towns*
Mostly built in the seventeenth and eighteenth centuries, in a geometrical layout with build-ing styles copied from Greek and Roman times.

Map 22

Photo 18

Phase 4 *Industrial Revolution towns*
Dating from the eighteenth and nineteenth centuries, these have many terraced houses crowded together alongside mills, mines and factories.

Map 23

Photo 19

Phase 5 *Modern towns*
Designed in the twentieth cen-tury for buses and cars to link shopping centres, housing estates and industrial areas.

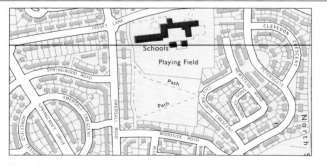
Map 24

Photo 20

The Romans were the first people to build townships in Britain. Their towns were small, compact settlements surrounded by a wall (W) and entered by large gates (G) and usually sited next to a river (R) which could be used by small ships. They unloaded at a quayside (Q). The centre of the town was a meeting square called a forum (Fm). Inside the town would be a fort (Ft). The streets would be laid out in a planned system. The river could be crossed by bridge (B) or ferry (Fy). Outside the town would be squatter-settlements (S) of unplanned shacks for house slaves, casual workers, etc.

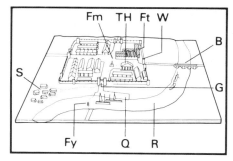

Fig. 26

After the Romans left Britain, towns declined in importance until the twelfth century. Between about 1100 and 1600 many market towns grew up. They had walls (W), a castle (Ca) and a market square (MS). The buildings were made of local stone and timber, and were in a crowded, unplanned layout, with narrow, winding streets. There were many churches (Ch) and a number of civic buildings such as a town hall (TH) and a Guild-hall (GH). Like Roman towns, medieval towns were built beside rivers (R) with a bridging-point (B).

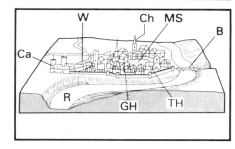

Fig. 27

After about 1600, towns expanded beyond the confines of their walls and spread out on to new ground. Larger stone or brick houses (SH) were built, sometimes with several floors. They were laid out in geometrical street layouts, such as crescents (Cr). Wealthy districts had gardens (G) and parks (P) as well as churches (Ch) and town halls (TH). Poorer people lived in small cottages with few amenities. Many of the better houses of this period survive as hotels, offices, surgeries, etc.

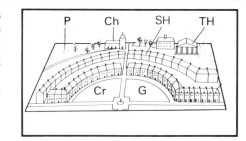

Fig. 28

The Industrial Revolution encouraged the large-scale growth of towns after 1800. As people generally walked to work, the factories (F) and mills (M) were close to the workers' terraced houses (Te). The industries were supplied by canals (C) and later by railways (Ry). Canals had locks (L) to change levels and wharfs (CW) for unloading goods. The largest growth of towns was on coalfield areas, where coal-mines (CM) were a dominant feature of the landscape. Other notable features were chapels (Ch) and large houses (LH) occupied by mine-, factory- and mill-owners. Note the high-density, straight-line pattern of the terraced rows.

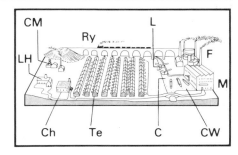

Fig. 29

Twentieth-century town growth has been spectacular because of the new mobility brought about by motorized road transport. This enabled people to live in housing estates (HE) separate from industrial estates (IE). The housing estates have curved streets (CS) and mostly detached (DH) and semi-detached (SDH) houses with gardens and garages. There is a lot of public open space (POS). Some people live in high-rise flats (HRF). There are suburban shopping parades (SSP).

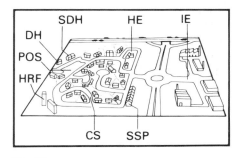

Fig. 30

ZONES OF A TOWN

Apart from new towns (for example, Milton Keynes) and towns that grew up during the Industrial Revolution, most urban areas have developed over many centuries and so have had many different phases of growth. A very simple but useful way to identify these phases of growth is to assume the town plan is like a cross-section through a tree trunk, with rings extending from the oldest growth in the middle to the youngest near the edge. Of course, some of the old buildings in the centre may have been knocked down to make way for modern commercial developments. Sometimes towns grow in sectors (like fingers) alongside railways, canals, rivers or main roads. Some sectors may be largely industrial, others filled with high-density, low-cost housing, others with a scattering of low-density, high-cost housing.

Below is a model diagram of a 'growth-ring' town pattern. Compare it with Map 25 and Fig. 32.

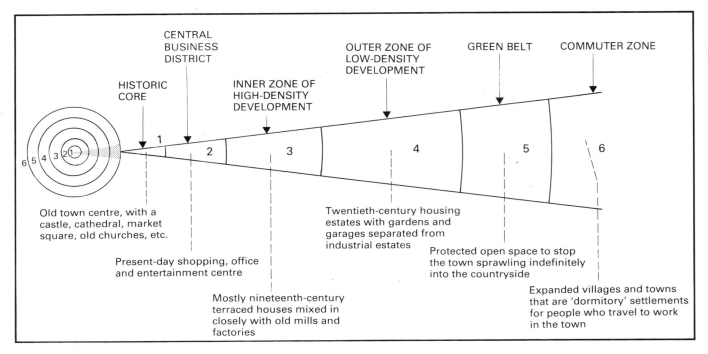

Fig. 31   *'Growth-ring' town pattern*

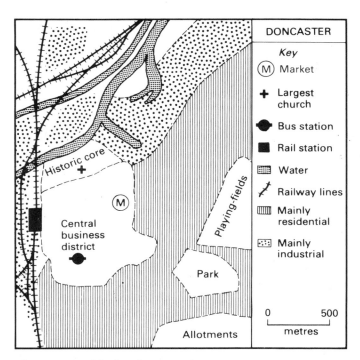

Fig. 32   *Simplified outline map of Map 25*

Exercise 14

1. *The OS map of Doncaster (Map 25) is drawn to a scale of 1:10 000, as are the maps on page 24. What extra information is available to us at this scale that is not shown on a 1:50 000 map (as on page 23)?*
2. *Describe the locations of the housing, business and residential sectors of Doncaster.*
3. *What sort of housing is most common in this part of Doncaster?*
4. *What recreational facilities are available in this part of town?*
5. *In which zones are the following streets:*
   (a) High Street (south of market)
   (b) Ravensworth Road (west of Elmfield Park)
   (c) Auckland Road (north of playing-fields)
   (d) Church View (near largest church)

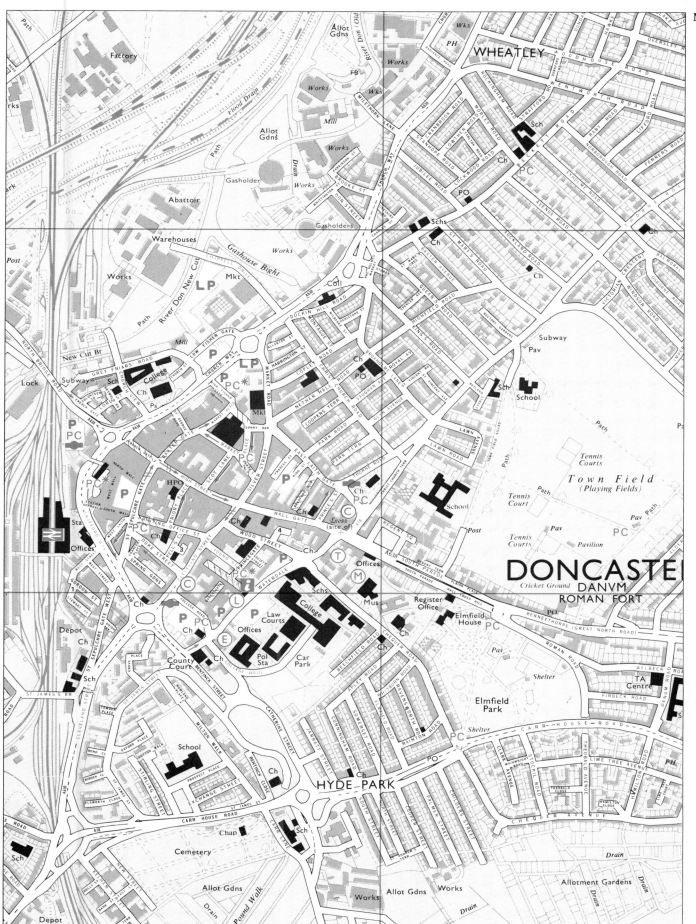

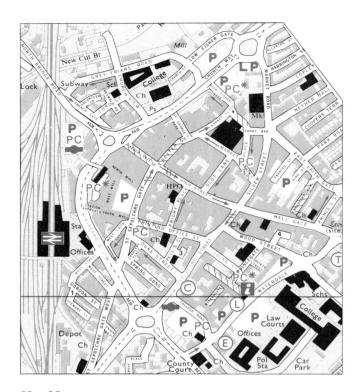

Map 26

The **central business district** (or CBD) is the commercial heart of a town or city. Often the CBD develops from the 'historic core' around a market and a town hall. In the town centre rents are very high, and this is reflected in two main ways. First, there are few houses, but many shops and offices. Second, many of the buildings are closely packed together and are often many storeys high. Often there are different zones within the CBD. These may include:

1. A *high-rent shopping area* mostly occupied by nationwide chain stores such as Boots, Marks & Spencer and Woolworth.
2. An *office and business area,* with banks, building societies, solicitors, etc.
3. A *market area,* with cheaper goods sold from stalls.
4. An area of smaller, more *specialist shops.* This area is often on the edge of the CBD where rents are lower.
5. An *educational area,* with colleges, museums, etc.
6. *Transport areas,* with rail and bus stations, multi-storey car-parks, etc.

Many changes are now taking place in the CBD's of our towns. Enclosed shopping precincts are now replacing the old high-street shops built along busy streets. Roads are being 'pedestrianized' (by banning motor traffic) or made into one-way systems. Large new furniture, D.I.Y. and food stores out of town are competing with the shops in the CBD.

Exercise 15
1. *Use Map 26 to find streets that are examples of each of the six different CBD zones listed above.*
2. *Describe the types of shops shown in the photo of the High Street (Photo 21).*
3. *Describe the CBD of your local town or city and contrast it with Doncaster.*

OS Ordnance Survey
DONCASTER
Town Map
Scale 1:10 000

RECREATION

(E) Swimming Bath
(M) Museum
(L) Library
(S) Sports Centre
(T) Theatre
(C) Cinema
⚑ Golf Course

ABBREVIATIONS

Ch	Church
FB	Foot Bridge
Mus	Museum
Pol Sta	Police Station
PO	Post Office
TH	Town Hall
Sch	School
Hosp	Hospital
TCB	Telephone Call Box

SERVICES

🛈 Information Centre
🚌 Bus/Coach Station
🚉 Railway Station
P Parking
LP Lorry Park
PC Public Convenience
PC✱ Public Convenience with facilities for disabled

ROUTE RESTRICTIONS
(Some may not apply at all times or to all vehicles)

One way traffic routes
One way traffic routes with restricted entry
No access in direction shown
Pedestrians only

Fig. 33 *Symbols used on OS 1:10 000 maps*

Photo 21 *High Street, in Doncaster's CBD*

Doncaster, like many towns, grew rapidly in the nineteenth century, thanks especially to the influence of the railways. Workers in the new factories and mills were housed in straight streets of closely packed terraced houses, as typified in the television programme *Coronation Street*. These houses have little or no garden space, and no built-in garage facilities.

The pattern on the map (as seen around Jubilee Road, for example) is quite unmistakable. Notice how these terraced houses are very close to the works on the opposite side of Church Way. The houses were built before the days of cars and buses, when most people had to walk to work. Notice too (on Map 25) that there are allotment gardens near to these terraced houses for residents who want to grow flowers and vegetables, but who do not have a large garden attached to their house. In some inner-city areas terraced houses have been knocked down and replaced by high-rise blocks of flats or by low-rise linked houses.

Map 27

Exercise 16

1. *Sometimes terraced houses of the Jubilee Road type have been demolished. What type of homes have replaced them in inner-city areas?*
2. *What type of shops are often found in these town environments?*
3. *Describe what you can see in the photograph of Jubilee Road and compare it with the information about this road given in Map 27. What does the map show better than the photograph? In what ways is the photograph more useful?*

Photo 22　*An inner-city environment (Jubilee Road, Doncaster)*

Photo 23   *A suburban housing estate (Atholl Crescent, Doncaster)*

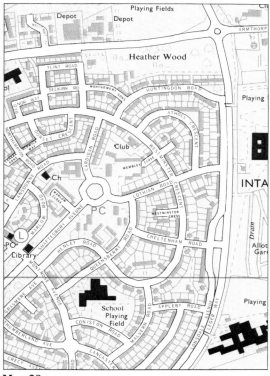

Map 28

After the First World War, planners and builders tried to break away from the terraced-street layout by laying out housing estates with curved roads and green open spaces. The houses themselves were often constructed as *detached* (single) or *semi-detached* (paired) homes with gardens at the front and back. Often garage space was provided too. This new 'suburban' layout required a lot more land than the old terraced streets, so towns grew up very rapidly (planners say 'sprawled') after 1920. The greater distances to school, work and shops created by spacing out the houses in this way meant that people had to travel by bus, car or bicycle rather than walk. Indeed, the availability of road transport meant that the houses could be built away from factories in a more pleasant 'estate' setting. Industries themselves became concentrated in industrial estates near main roads and railway lines.

Exercise 17

1. *Find Atholl Crescent on Map 28. Imagine that you live in one of the semi-detached houses and a friend lives in Jubilee Road (see Map 27). Compare your house and your street with those of your friend.*
2. *Compare the street names on Maps 27 and 28.*
3. *Compare the provision of open spaces and the location of schools in Maps 27 and 28.*
4. *What sort of shops are likely to be found in the area shown on Map 28? Where might they be located?*

We have already seen that there is far more open space in suburban town environments than in inner-city environments. Yet, as the three photographs show, there are some large and important parts of the inner zone of Doncaster that are not built up.

Many people look for recreational space just outside the town on the *urban fringe*. Around Doncaster, for example, are parks, golf-courses, cricket grounds, picnic sites, an airfield and a racecourse. Also on the edge of town, the urban area imposes on the countryside in many essential, but unpleasant, ways. There are sewage works, rubbish-tips and quarries for building materials.

Often people choose to live outside the town and to travel to their factory or office each day by train, bus or car. These people are called *commuters* and many towns have commuter housing estates attached to villages situated beyond the edge of town. Some people call these *dormitory settlements*. Can you suggest why?

To protect the open countryside around a town from being built on, planners have made a ring zone called a *green belt* in which new developments are strictly controlled.

Photo 24
Open space: playing-fields

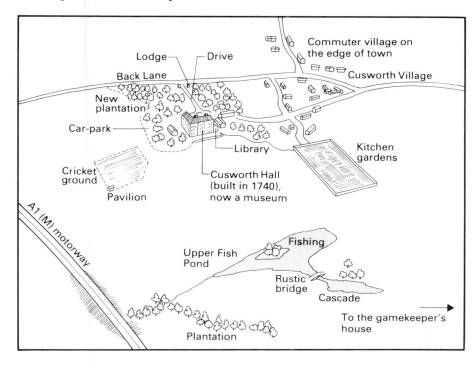

Fig. 34 *Diagram showing some of the amenities of Cusworth Park, a public open space on the north-west side of Doncaster, about 4 kilometres from the town centre*

Photo 25
Open space: cemetery

Exercise 18

1. *Fig. 34 shows part of Cusworth Park, which lies west of Doncaster near the A1(M) Doncaster Bypass. What amenities are provided here for the residents of the town to come out to enjoy?*
2. *Map 57 (page 87) shows the urban fringe of the city of Liverpool. Describe how the open land is used.*
3. *Look carefully at the three photographs on this page. One was taken near Carr House Road, one near Chequer Avenue and one near Bennetthorpe. Using Map 25 (page 27), suggest where each photograph was taken. Try to locate the spot where the photographer stood as precisely as possible.*

Photo 26
Open space: allotments

ROADS AND RAILWAYS

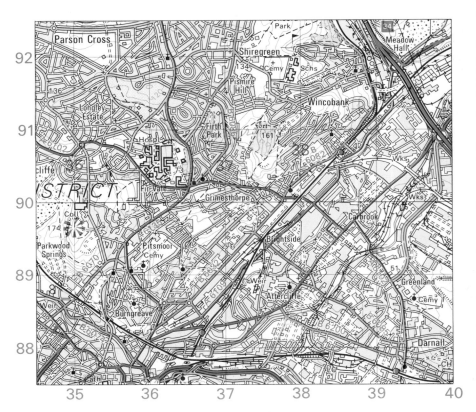

Map 29

Exercise 19

1. *Map 29 shows part of Sheffield.*
   (a) *Make a larger sketch-map of the railway layout, with labels to show all the features, such as tunnels, stations and viaducts. (Use page 4 to help you.)*
   (b) *How many of the types of roads shown on page 4 can you spot on this map?*
2. *Fig. 35 is a diagram of an imaginary landscape with railways and roads. Fig. 36 is a partly drawn map of the same landscape. Trace and complete Fig. 36, using only 1:50 000 scale conventional signs.*

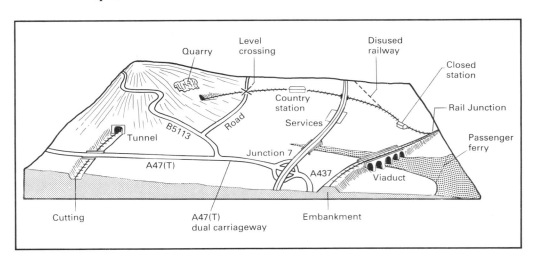

Fig. 35

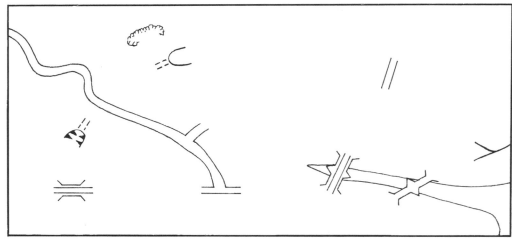

Fig. 36

Whether rocks were formed from molten material cooling from high temperatures *(igneous rocks)*, from the remains of plants, animals and rock particles *(sedimentary rocks)*, or from alteration by heat and pressure *(metamorphic rocks)*, the scenery that these rocks create is largely the result of two qualities. One quality is **permeability.** As we briefly mentioned on page 16, some rocks allow water to sink through, while others don't. *Permeable* rocks let water soak down from the surface, with the result that there may be few streams or rivers flowing over these rocks. Some permeable rocks, like chalk, are porous (water sinks through pores in the rock). Some, like limestone, are pervious (water sinks mostly through cracks and joints). *Impermeable* rocks have a lot of surface water, including lakes, marshes and peaty ground as well as rivers.

The second key quality of a rock is its **hardness.** Some rocks, like granite, are extremely tough and so form rugged landscapes with steep slopes and high ground. Other rocks (such as clay or sand) are very soft, and so form gently sloping lowland. Rocks that are hard and not easily eroded are called *resistant* rocks.

When we look at landscapes on maps we must ask ourselves whether we can see a lot of *surface water* or not, and whether the land is *rugged* or *smooth*.

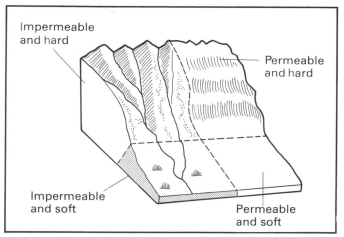

Fig. 37

Exercise 20

1. *Look at Fig. 38. Arrange these rocks in descending order of resistance to erosion: sandstone, gravel, shale, granite.*
2. *Look at the maps listed below. Try to work out the possible rock type present in each one by examining the density of rivers and streams (to give permeability) and the number of contours present (suggesting resistance):*
   Map 3 (page 8)   Map 4 (page 12)   Map 6 (page 12)
   Map 7 (page 12)   Map 14 (page 19)   Map 16 (page 19)

Fig. 38   *Graph showing rock permeability and hardness*

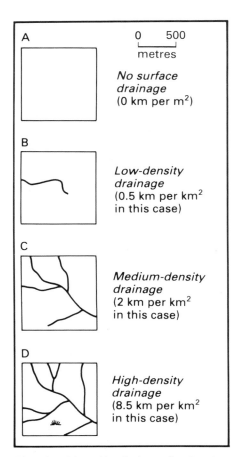

Fig. 39 *Measuring drainage density. A suggests very permeable rock, D very impermeable rock.*

Exercise 21

1. *Look at Map 30 and calculate the drainage-density figures for squares 1381, 1583 and 1288.*
2. *Which squares in Question 1 are on permeable rock? Which are on impermeable rock?*
3. *Use the geological map (Fig. 40) to name the rock type in each of the three squares.*
4. *Use the graph on the previous page to put the three rocks named in question 3 in order of permeability. Start with the most permeable.*

Remember that while permeable rocks have few surface streams and rivers, the opposite is true for impermeable rocks. One way to check this out on an OS map is to take a sample number of 1-kilometre grid squares and measure the total length of rivers and streams in each square. This provides a very rough-and-ready indicator of the *stream density*.

To measure the length of a winding feature such as a river, take a straight-edged piece of scrap paper, and put a mark at each point where you pivot the paper to follow a change in direction. When you have pivoted your way round all the bends, read off the final length against a scale line (see page 6). Alternatively, you could use a piece of thread or a pair of dividers to measure the length of rivers in grid squares.

While you are examining the stream densities, you may also be interested in observing *stream patterns*. Some streams join main rivers just like twigs joining branches of a tree. This is called a *dendritic pattern*. Sometimes streams run *parallel* to each other. Others spread out in a *radial pattern* from a dome-shaped hill to give a hub-and-spoke layout on a map. Some rivers have a lot of short side-tributaries, which give a *feather pattern*. The diagrams on page 41 show these patterns clearly.

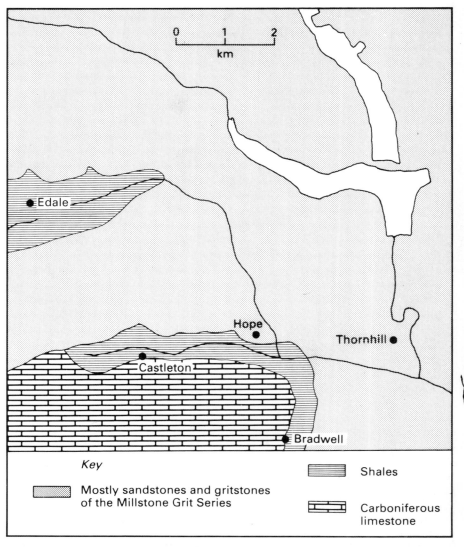

Fig. 40 *Simplified geological sketch-map of Map 30*

Exercise 22

Use all the data on pages 33–35 when answering these questions about Map 30.

1. *Why do you think Ladybower Reservoir was constructed where it is? (Hints: rock permeability, valley shape, settlement, rainfall.)*

2. *Suggest some social problems that would arise if the River Noe were dammed at Edale End (163863).*

3. *Limestone is used for making cement, for roadstone and in steel-making. List the likely good and bad effects on the local area of quarrying limestone south-east of Castleton.*

4. *What map evidence is there that limestone rock develops interesting underground features?*

5. *Comment on the drainage patterns of*
   (a) *the streams draining from Blackden Edge (square 1288)*
   (b) *the tributaries of the River Noe (1485 and 1586)*
   (c) *the streams draining from Win Hill (1885).*

ROCKS: RESISTANCE TO EROSION

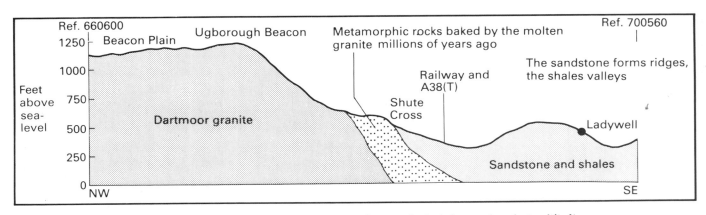

Fig. 41   Sketch section from 660600 to 700560 on Map 31, showing basic geological changes (much simplified)

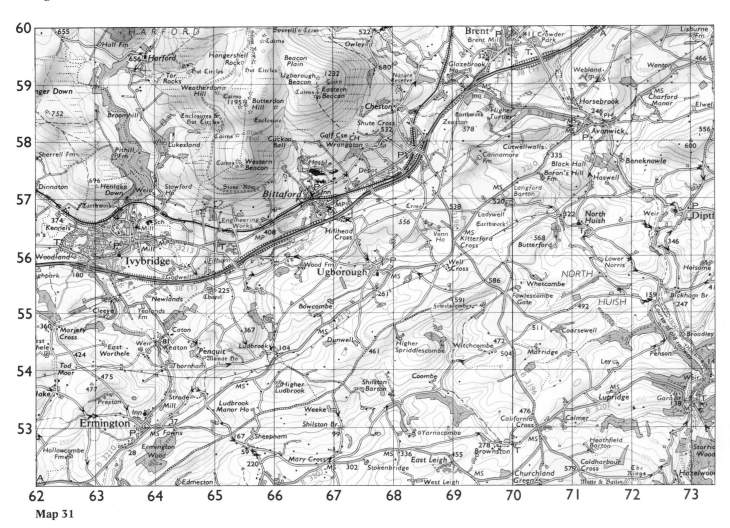

Map 31

Exercise 23

Map 31 is an extract from one of the most attractive and colourful OS maps, the 1:63 360 scale tourist map of Dartmoor. This odd-sounding representative fraction stems from the fact that the scale of the map is 1 inch to 1 mile (63 360 inches in one mile). This tourist map is one of the few non-metric maps still published. It has been chosen for this section because the hill shading and colouring bring out the relief of the area so well.

1. (a) Using the map and the diagram, estimate the average height of the granite moorland.

(b) How does this differ from the metamorphic rocks and sandstones?

2. (a) What do you notice about the shapes of the hills south and east of the A38(T)?

(b) How does this pattern of alternating hills and valleys (caused by alternating beds of harder sandstones and softer shales tilted at an angle to the horizontal) affect the road layout?

3. What conclusions can you draw about the effects of rock resistance on landscapes?

Photo 27   *Dartmoor granite landscape*

Photo 28   *Devonian sandstone scenery*

Exercise 24

1. *Look carefully at the granite area which lies to the north of the railway line.*

   (a) *Why do you think this area has been set aside as a National Park? (The National Park boundary is shown by a broad yellow dashed line on this map.)*

   (b) *What evidence is there to suggest that there were more settlements on the granite area in prehistoric times than today? Why should this be? (Hint: think about the extent of woodland cover before the Roman occupation, and consider just how hard it would have been for early man to cut down trees.)*

   (c) *What facilities are provided for visitors to the Dartmoor National Park in this area?*

2. *Comment on the reasons for the distribution of woods and forests on this map extract.*

3. *What could you say about the site of the settlements of Ivybridge, Brent and Ermington? (You may find it helpful to revise from pages 18 and 19.)*

4. *'Granite is an acid rock and, as such, produces very poor-quality, acid soils. This means the soil is rich in silica, and deficient in lime. The soils on the sandstones and shales of the lower land are much richer in lime, and are therefore far more fertile.'*

   What evidence can you see on the map to support this comment? What else, besides soil acidity, makes the granite land infertile?

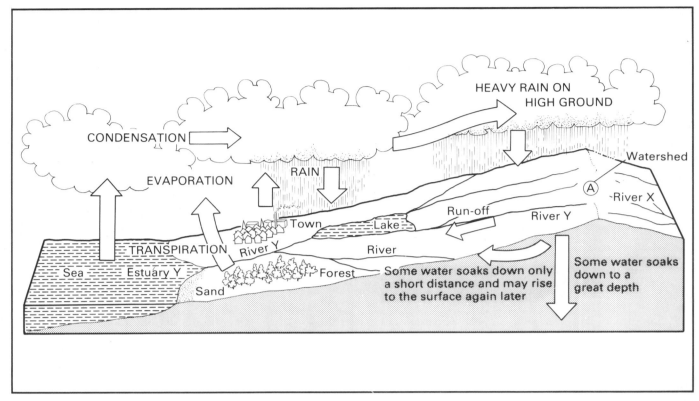

Fig. 42 *The hydrological cycle: how water circulates from the sea to the land and back again*

Air passing over sea areas will pick up moisture by *evaporation*. As this moist air moves inland, some of that moisture will be dropped as *precipitation*. This complex-sounding name includes rain, snow, hail, drizzle, dew, etc. For simplicity's sake, we will refer to it simply as 'rain'. In general, rainfall is greater on hills and mountains, because the water vapour in the air is forced to cool, and so to condense, as it rises to cross high land.

When a raindrop hits the ground, it may do one of three things. It could *evaporate* back into the air (notice how puddles soon dry up when the sun comes out). It could *soak into the ground* (remember that the permeability of the rock (page 34) greatly affects how much rainfall soaks underground). It could *run off* to join a stream, river or lake, and perhaps flow back into the sea again.

Far more rain runs off from a bare hillside than from a forested one. Far more rain runs off from the streets of a town than from sand-dunes. Can you explain why?

If a raindrop lands at A in Fig. 42 and doesn't soak in or evaporate, it will flow into either river X or river Y. This dividing line (like the ridge on the roof of a house) is called a *watershed*. All the rivers and streams that drain into the sea at estuary Y are in the *drainage basin* of river Y. The edge of a drainage basin is always a watershed.

If the raindrop does soak into the ground, it may go deep down *(infiltration)* or may stay near the surface, perhaps to re-emerge later as a spring *(storage)*.

Exercise 25

1. *Locate the clapper bridge on the River Avon at 657663 on Map 32. Find out the height above sea-level of this bridge (remember that this is still part of the Dartmoor Tourist Map, so the contours are in feet, and the scale of the map is 1 inch to 1 mile – 1 kilometre is 0·62 miles, and 1 mile is 1·61 kilometres).*

2. *(a) Follow the River Avon upstream to its source. How and where does it rise, and at what height?*

    (b) The footpath called Sandy Way crosses the watershed of the Avon somewhere in square 6469. Give a six-figure reference for the point on the path where you think the watershed is.

3. *Why do you think the Avon Dam reservoir is well placed to catch a lot of rainwater?*

4. *Look at the flood hydrographs. Fig. 43.1 explains what each of them shows. Fig. 43.2 shows how the flow of water in the Avon at the clapper bridge responds to a day of heavy rainfall. A second recording-station set up on the Holy Brook as it enters Buckfastleigh plots a different hydrograph pattern for the same day.*

    (a) In what way are the two river run-off rates different?

    (b) Remembering all the points raised on these two pages and what you learned about the contrasts between the granite upland and the sandstone lowland (pages 36–7), explain why the two rivers react differently to the same wet day.

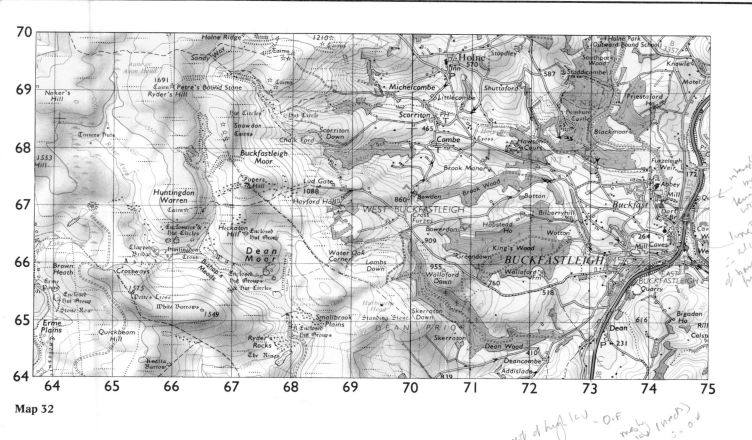

Map 32

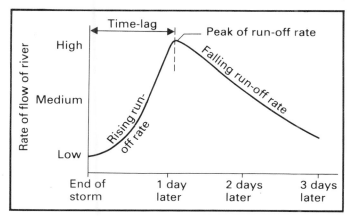

Fig. 43.1 *This is a flood hydrograph. It shows the changes in the flow of a river after a day of very heavy rain. There is a time-lag between the rain falling and reaching the river, so the run-off rate reaches its peak a day after the end of the storm.*

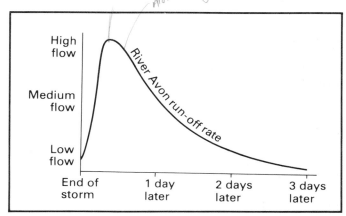

Fig. 43.2 *Flood hydrograph for the River Avon at the clapper bridge (657663) after a heavy storm*

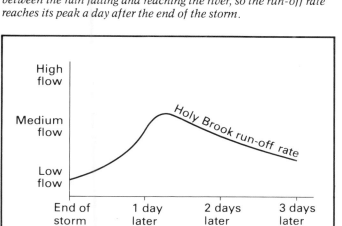

Fig. 43.3 *Flood hydrograph for Holy Brook, Buckfastleigh (730663) after the same storm*

DRAINAGE BASINS

Photo 29 *From the air, these drainage patterns show up very clearly. Can you see the watersheds?*

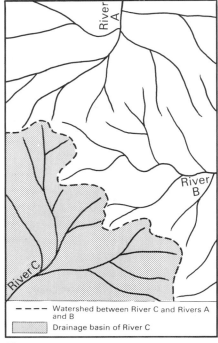

- - - - Watershed between River C and Rivers A and B

▒ Drainage basin of River C

Fig. 44

We have already briefly introduced the idea of watersheds and drainage basins. Now let's explore them in more detail.

The photograph shows a mountain area in the western U.S.A. taken from an altitude of 10 kilometres. Because there is very little settlement or forestry in the area shown, the river valleys stand out clearly. We can see where the tributaries begin, and where the watersheds between one major valley and another are.

Fig. 44 shows part of a landscape similar to that in the photograph. The dotted line shows the watershed between river C and rivers A and B. The shaded area shows the drainage basin (or *catchment area*) of river C. All rainfall that runs off in this shaded area will eventually flow into river C.

Exercise 26
1. (a) *Make a copy of Fig. 44.*
   (b) *Mark in the watershed between rivers A and B.*
   (c) *Shade the drainage basins of rivers A and B in different colours.*
2. *Draw an imaginary island with a volcano in the centre. Add rivers flowing to the sea. Draw the watersheds and colour in the drainage basins of each river.*

40

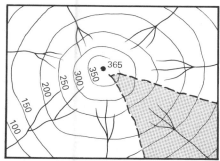

Fig. 45.1 Radial *drainage pattern.* *Drainage basins of rivers flowing in a radial pattern from a dome-shaped hill.*

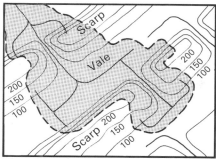

Fig. 45.2 Trellis *drainage pattern.* *Complex-shaped drainage basin on alternating bands of hard and soft rock which have been gently tilted to the south-east, giving a scarp-and-vale landscape (scarps are hills with one steep side and one gently sloping side).*

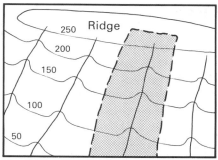

Fig. 45.3 Parallel *drainage pattern.* *Parallel rivers with long, narrow drainage basins flowing off a ridge.*

Map 33

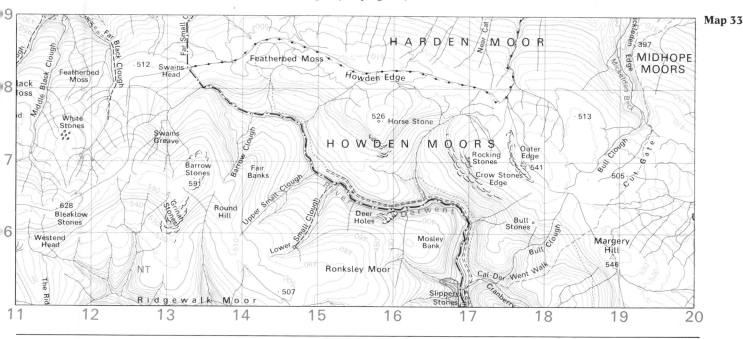

Exercise 27

Drainage basins vary a great deal in size and shape. The most important reason for this is the shape of the land (the relief). You may remember the section about relief features on pages 12 and 13. Figs. 45.1, 45.2 and 45.3 show three very differently shaped drainage basins, associated with a dome-shaped hill (like a large knoll), a scarp-and-vale landscape, and a ridge.

1. *What shape of drainage basins could we expect to find for rivers draining off (a) a plateau, and (b) a spur? Answer by means of two drawings.*
2. *(a) Using Map 33, suggest where you might go if you wanted to find the source of the River Derwent.*
   (b) By placing a piece of tracing-paper over this map, try to draw in the watershed between the drainage basins of the Derwent and the other rivers on this map. The map is a 1:50 000 OS map with contours drawn in metres above sea-level.
3. *Geographers sometimes talk about stream orders. A first-order stream is a small stream flowing from its source without any tributaries. The stream below the junction of two first-order streams is a second-order stream. The river only becomes of third-order rank once another second-order stream joins it, not when another first-order stream joins. A fourth-order river occurs when two third-order rivers merge, and so on. What order is the River Derwent at Slippery Stones?*

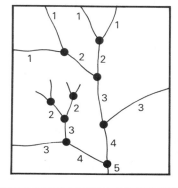

Fig. 46 *Dendritic drainage.* *Stream orders:* *1=first-order stream,* *2=second-order stream, etc.*

RIVER VALLEYS

River valleys may be grouped into three types:

1. **Without a flood plain**
   Flood plains are flat areas of silt, sand, mud and gravel deposited by the flood-waters of a river. In some stages of a river's course, it is so busily engaged in cutting downwards that the sides of the valley are too steep for a flood plain to form. In these cases a deep, V-shaped valley is formed, with the features shown in Fig. 47 and Photo 30 (below).

2. **With flood plains on one side of the valley only**
   At some points along a river's course, it deposits silt on the insides of its meanders (bends) but keeps eroding into solid bedrock on the outsides of the bends. As the river winds along towards the sea a small flood plain appears first on one bank and then on the other.

3. **With wide flood plains on both sides**
   These valleys are characterized by deposition on both sides of the meander bends. The flood plain is sometimes many kilometres wide.

Valley type 1 usually occurs near the source of the river and type 3 near the mouth, but it is fairly common for a river to have a wide flood plain in some parts of its upper course, or to pass through a gorge near the sea.

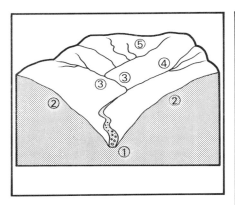

Fig. 47   *Features of a river with no flood plain:*
1. Narrow river flowing through boulders and pebbles, like a torrent.
2. Steep, V-shaped valley sides going right down to the river.
3. Interlocking spurs (like the interlocked fingers of two hands).
4. Many tributaries.
5. Waterfalls and rapids are common.

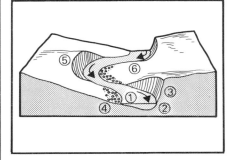

Fig. 48   *Features of a river with flood plains on one side only:*
1. River flows fastest on outside of meander.
2. River is deepest on outside of bend.
3. River bank undercut by strong current, creating river cliffs.
4. Silt, sand and mud deposited by slack water on inside of bend.
5. Steep slope of valley.
6. Gentle slope of valley.

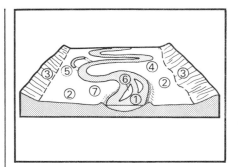

Fig. 49   *Features of a river with flood plains on both sides:*
1. Wide, silty river flowing down a gentle gradient.
2. Wide flood plain on both sides of river.
3. Bluff-line marks edge of flood plain.
4. Large meanders.
5. Cut-off or abandoned meander with ox-bow lake.
6. Silty islands (called eyots) show that braiding is taking place.
7. These raised silty banks (called levées) form during times of flood.

Photo 30   *A river without a flood plain*

Photo 31   *A river with a flood plain on one side only*

Photo 32   *A river with a wide flood plain*

Exercise 28

1. *Which of the three types of river valleys shown on the previous page can be found in the following squares on Map 34 (a 1:50 000 scale map of the Quantock Hills in Somerset)?*

   (a) *1240*
   (b) *0842*
   (c) *1542*

2. *Make an enlargement of each of the squares listed above. In each case, sketch in the contour patterns and the course of the river.*

3. *The drawing on page 36 is a sketch section across the southern edge of Dartmoor and its surrounding lowland.*

The sketch section is like a graph, with horizontal distance on the X-axis and vertical distance on the Y-axis. Try drawing similar sketch sections along the following grid lines

   (a) *grid line 12 of square 1240*
   (b) *grid line 42 of square 0842*
   (c) *grid line 42 of square 1542.*

   (Accurate sections could be made using graph paper to plot exact horizontal and vertical distances from one end of the line of section to the other.)

   How do your sketch sections compare with the fronts of the three block diagrams on page 42?

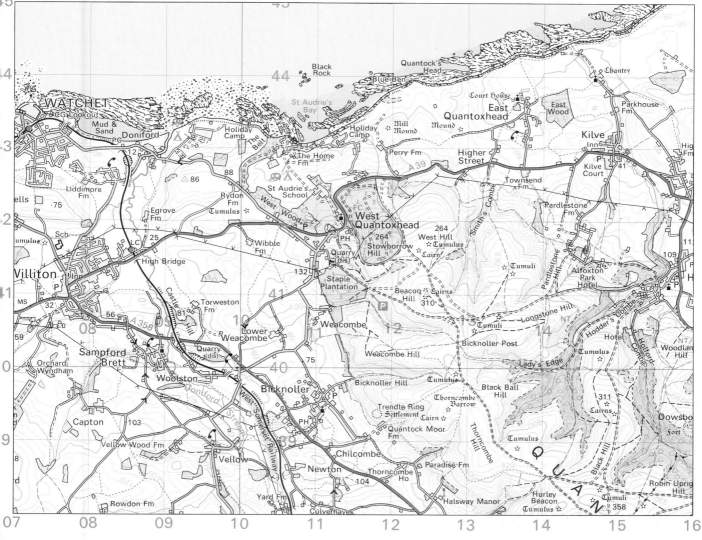

Map 34

CONTRASTING COASTLINES

Exercise 29
With the help of Fig. 50, identify each of the fifteen features shown in Fig. 51.

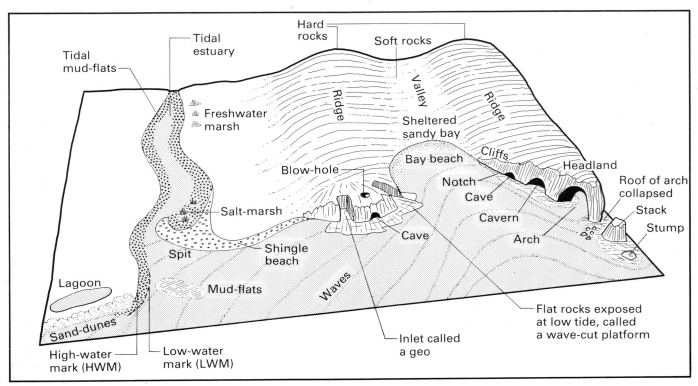

Fig. 50   *Common coastal features*

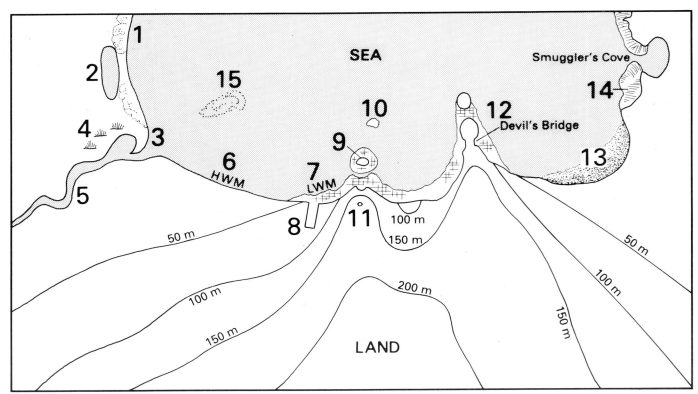

Fig. 51   *Sketch-map of an imaginary coastal area*

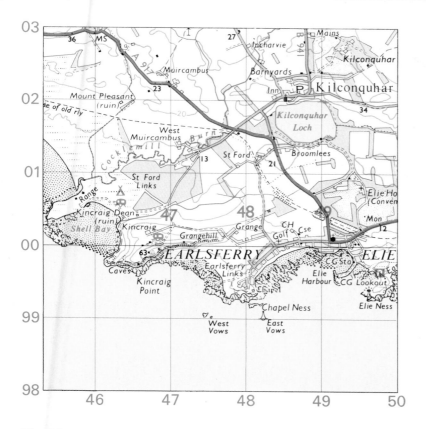

Map 35

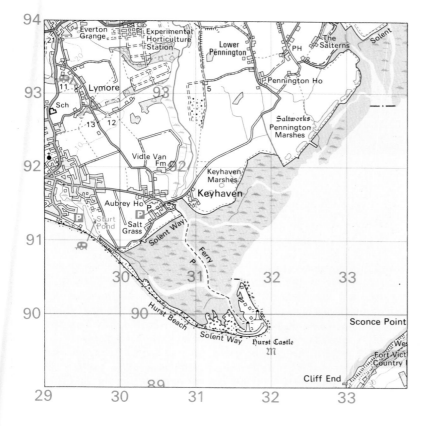

Map 36

Exercise 30

1. *Complete this statement about Map 35 (a 1:50 000 map of the Fife coastline in eastern Scotland) by filling in the missing letters and words:*

   'Although most of the coastline has f........ ....s exposed at low tide, the western end around Shell Bay has ....and..........on view when the tide goes out. Except for Shell Bay, the coastline is one where e..........n is taking place. There are .... at West Vows and East Vows. The lighthouse occupies a h.......... site. The highest cliffs are .... metres high.'

2. *Map 36 shows the famous Hurst Castle Spit in Hampshire (also on a 1:50 000 scale). Complete the following description of this section of coastline:*

   'Hurst Castle is at the end of a spit made of .... which is about .... kilometres long. It is possible to see at least .... traces of former positions of the spit, before it became as large as it is at present. You can see that the waves come in from the ...., because most of the deposition is on the sheltered .... side. North-east of the spit are extensive s.......... m.........., as names like .... show. This coastline is very different from that shown in Map 35.

3. *Make a sketch of the coastline shown in Map 35. On your drawing, label as many of the features shown in Fig. 50 as you can identify.*

CONTRASTING COASTLINES

Photo 33   *Lindisfarne, Northumberland, from the air*

Exercise 31

The photograph shows part of Lindisfarne on Holy Island, Northumberland. The remains of the priory can be seen between the village and the ridge of harder rock that runs parallel to the shore. This resistant rock is an igneous type called dolerite that was once injected underground in a molten state into cracks in layers of older sedimentary rocks. Geologists call this feature a dyke.

Today the covering layers of rock have been eroded away to reveal the dolerite on the surface. It is visibly harder than the surrounding sedimentary rocks. The ridge that it forms is known on Holy Island as the Heugh. The harbour in the
foreground is called the Oose, and if you look very carefully, you can see a line of old, low cliffs. These tell us that sea-level has changed in the last few thousand years. You can see a wave-cut platform attached to the Heugh, and in the background are the tidal Holy Island Sands. You can just see part of a stack on the extreme left of the picture.

With the help of the photograph, draw a sketch-map of this part of Holy Island. Wherever possible, use the correct conventional signs for coastal features for a 1:50 000 map (see page 4). Add labels to point out the features mentioned in the description given above.

Ordnance Survey maps can help you get to know an area well. If you stand at a good viewpoint and match the scenery with a map you will find it easier to orient yourself and to work out where the hills, roads, villages, rivers and other features are in relation to each other. You will also find that you can identify different housing patterns, types of agriculture and so on.

In Exercise 32 we save your legs by taking you up to two different viewpoints overlooking Church Stretton in Shropshire. (Look at the map and the photos on pages 47 to 49.) The hills in this region are composed of Pre-Cambrian rocks, some of the oldest in Britain. The valley was created by powerful faults resulting from severe earthquakes long ago. The contrast between life in the sheltered valley and the exposed hilltops is dramatic. The valley contains most of the enclosed farmland, most of the settlement and the main routes that link Shrewsbury and Hereford.

Map 37 (on the following page) covers the Church Stretton area, and introduces another scale of OS map. It is drawn to the scale of 1:25 000. The 1-kilometre grid lines are therefore 40 mm apart, compared with the 20-mm distance for the 1:50 000 map that appears so frequently in the first section of this book. The 1:25 000 map uses different colours and some of the conventional signs are different too. Contours are drawn at 5-metre vertical intervals and field boundaries are shown.

Exercise 32

1. *What is the number of the main road on the floor of the valley?*
2. *What is the difference in height between this road and the spot on the summit of Caer Caradoc where Photo 34 was taken?*
3. *What is the name of the village in the photograph?*
4. *In which compass direction was the camera pointing?*
5. *What is the name of the valley leading from the village into the hills?*
6. *The hills in the picture, called The Long Mynd, have a very flat summit-level. What are such hills called?*
7. *Compare the way the land is used on either side of the B4370.*

Photo 34 *The Long Mynd Hills seen from Caer Caradoc*

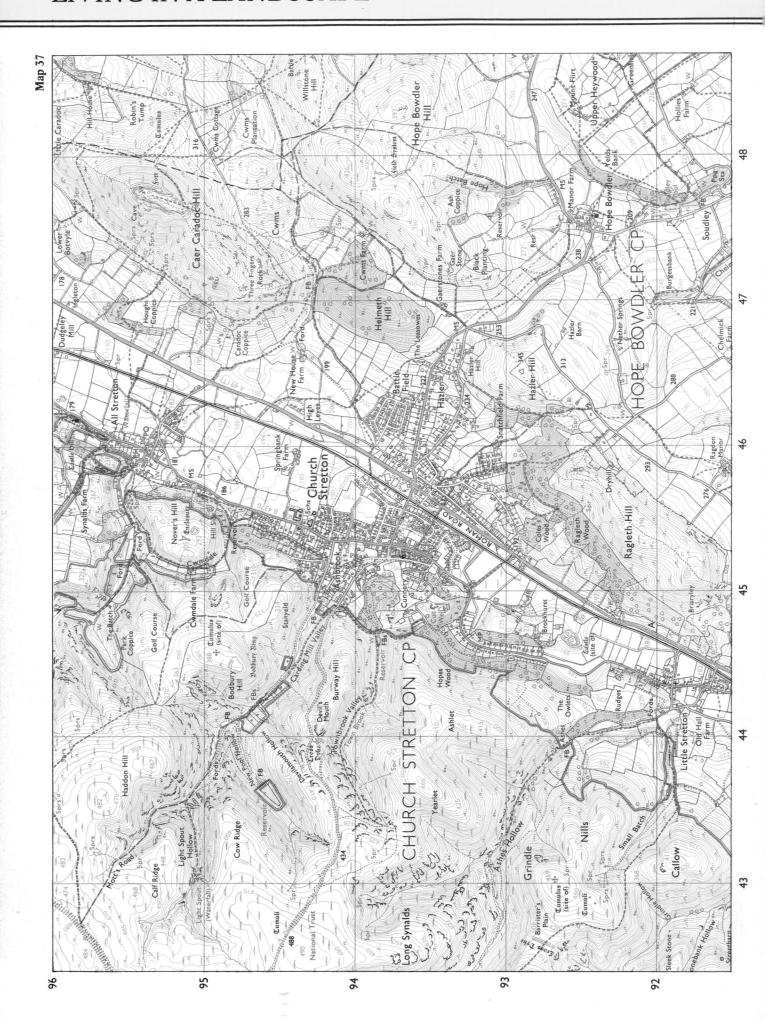

The A49(T) and the railway in Map 37 follow what geologists call a **rift-valley**. This is a trough created by *faults* (breaks caused by earthquakes thousands of years ago) running parallel to each other along the valley edges. Look at the rift-valley in Fig. 52 and Map 37. Describe the agriculture there.

To the west of the rift-valley lies The Long Mynd plateau, deeply cut into by V-shaped river valleys with steep sides and no flood plains. (Name five of these valleys.) The Long Mynd appears in Photo 34. What is the land mainly used for?

The eastern side of the rift-valley is dominated by Caer Caradoc Hill and other similarly shaped ridges (try to name three of these) formed from ancient volcanic lavas tilted so that they almost stand on end. There is a lot of rough pasture in this area and much of it is not enclosed by field boundaries.

Exercise 33

Fig. 52 is a block diagram of the Church Stretton area (see Map 37) drawn from west to east from square 4395 to 4895. Look carefully at the map and identify features A to M.

Fig. 52

THE LONG 'MYND

West — East

Metres above sea-level: 0, 200, 400, 500

Line 43, 44, 45, 46, 47, 48, 49, 95

Feature — A, B, C, D, E, F, G, H, I, J, K, L, M

Ridge

Track

Light Spout Hollow

The Batch Valley

Amenity

Water features

Type of woodland

Hill

Ancient monument

Mill

All Stretton

Ancient defence

Hole in the ground

Little Caradoc

Ancient burial-place

Caer Caradoc

ANCIENT PRE-CAMBRIAN ROCKS, MOSTLY VOLCANIC AND METAMORPHIC

SHALES

ANCIENT VOLCANIC ROCKS

Faults producing a rift-valley

Thin deposits of boulder clay from the ice-ages, and river silts

Photo 35   *View of the Church Stretton area from The Long Mynd (the range of hills on the western side of the map)*

THE EFFECTS OF THE ICE-AGES

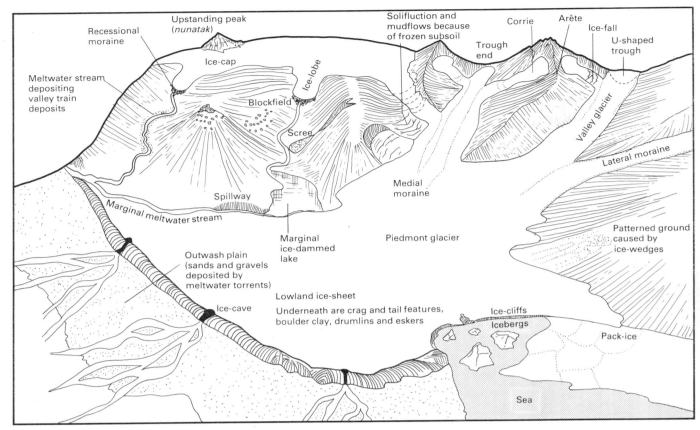

Fig. 53   *Glacial environments*

Within the last million years, Europe and North America have experienced at least four periods when temperatures were lower than today and the precipitation fell as snow, turned to ice, and failed to thaw during the summer. These times were called **ice-ages**.

As a result, *ice-caps* covered the tops of mountains and plateaux and spilled down to cover many of the lowlands with *ice-sheets*. Hollows and heads of valleys were filled with pockets of ice called *corries*. Ice flowed slowly downslope into mountain valleys to create *valley glaciers*.

We have seen how river valleys in mountains are usually V-shaped in cross-section (as on The Long Mynd). The power of glaciers is such that river valleys once occupied by ice were straightened, widened and deepened to form impressive *U-shaped troughs*.

Often these valley glaciers merged into *piedmont glaciers* and *lowland ice-sheets* when they reached the plains. Any ground left exposed, not covered with ice, was subject to severe *frosts* which shattered rocks and heaved up soil and debris into unusual patterns.

The ice-ages did more than cover much of the land with ice and heavy frosts. The weight of ice on the land caused subsidence, while the hydrological cycle (see page 38) was upset because the water was locked in glaciers and ice-sheets and did not return to the sea. Sea-level changed. The sea itself froze over to form *pack-ice*. Where glaciers and ice-sheets reached the sea, *icebergs* formed.

As the ice-ages came to an end and a *thaw* set in, huge *meltwater rivers* developed. These deposited layers of sands and gravels over a wide area. When the ice thinned and eventually vanished, a new landscape came into view. The lowlands were coated with deposits of angular stones mixed up with a sticky clay called *boulder clay*. At places where the margins of the ice-sheets had been, ridges of rubble called *moraines* were left. On mountainsides, where frost action had been very active, *shattered rocks* and fan-shaped piles of stones (called *screes*) were evident. Mountain valleys were *U-shaped*, with tributaries entering them half-way up the valley sides (called *hanging valleys*). Where the corries were, knife-edged ridges called *arêtes* were carved out. Where several corrie glaciers ate into a hilltop, a *pyramidal peak* resulted.

Coastal regions didn't escape the effects of the ice-ages either. The changes in sea-level left some places with *drowned estuaries* (V-shaped valleys) and *fjords* (drowned U-shaped valleys). In other places, as on Holy Island (see page 46), old *abandoned cliff-lines* and *raised beaches* appeared.

The effects of the ice-ages were far-reaching and complex. On pages 50 to 53 we explore some of the major features of glaciation found on many of the OS maps of Britain.

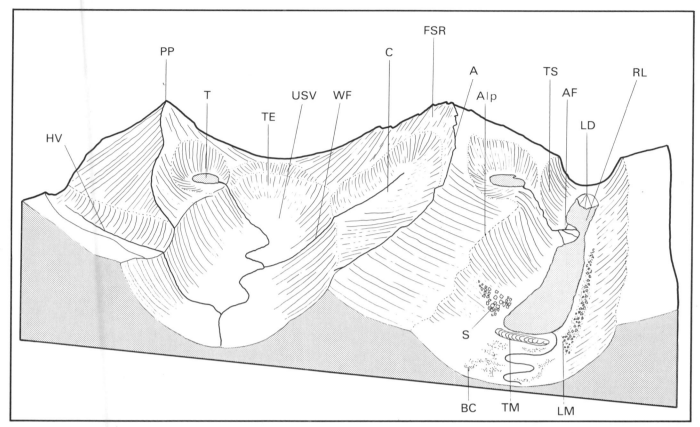

Fig. 54 *Diagram of the area in the top right-hand corner of Fig. 53 after the ice has thawed*

Photo 36 *Ice-sheets spreading into lowland areas from glaciated mountains, Greenland. This is what Britain would have looked like during the ice-ages.*

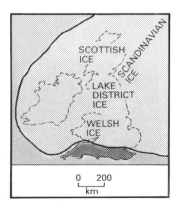

Fig. 55 *How Britain looked when ice-coverage was at its most extensive.*

Exercise 34

Write down the correct names for each of the labelled features in Fig. 54, choosing from the following list. (Names that have not appeared before are explained in brackets.) The first one has been done for you.

alluvial fan *(a fan-shaped deposit of silt at the foot of a gully)* = AF

alp *(a high, level bench or shoulder of gently sloping land)*

arête

boulder clay

corrie

frost-shattered rocks

hanging valley

lake delta

lateral moraine *(debris deposited by a glacier on the side of a valley)*

pyramidal peak

ribbon lake *(a long, narrow lake in the floor of a glaciated valley)*

scree

tarn *(a small lake in a corrie)*

terminal moraine *(rubble deposited across a valley by a stationary glacier)*

trough end of a glacial valley

truncated spur

U-shaped valley trough

waterfall

GLACIATED MOUNTAIN SCENERY

The Cuillin Hills on the Isle of Skye (in north-western Scotland) show the effects of ice-action in the most dramatic way. The glaciers in this part of the island were so powerful that they cut very deeply into the mountains. Many of the slopes are so steep that they cannot be shown by contour lines. What symbol has been used on Map 38 to show these very steep slopes?

The steep slopes and the extensive areas of bare rock and scree make walking and climbing in the Cuillin Hills exciting but dangerous. The Cuillin ridge is the most famous in British mountaineering.

Photo 37   *Sgurr Alasdair in the Cuillin Hills, Skye*

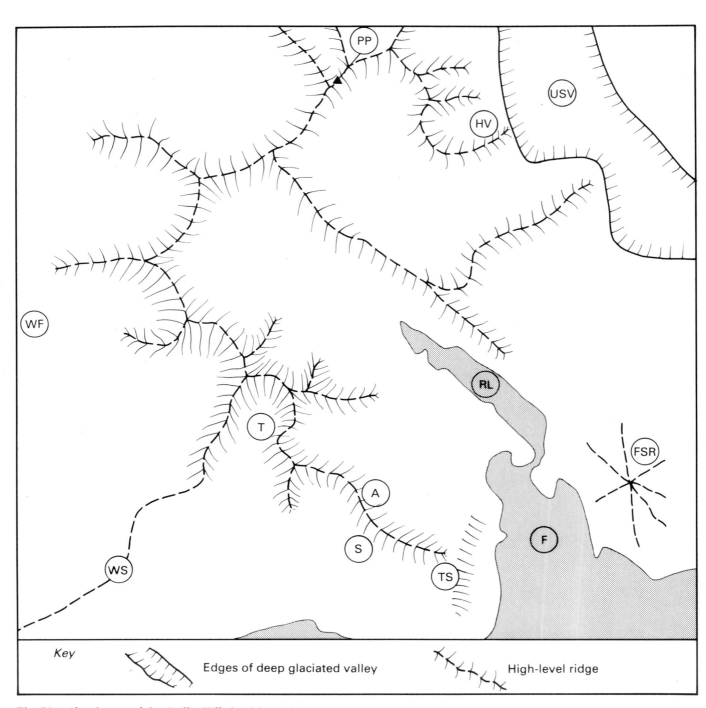

Key

~~~~~~~ Edges of deep glaciated valley

+++++++ High-level ridge

Fig. 56   *Sketch-map of the Cuillin Hills (see Map 38)*

Exercise 35

Using all the resources on pages 50–53, answer the following:

1. *Identify all the glacial features shown in Fig. 56. (If you are stumped by the feature labelled* **WS** *turn to page 40;* **F** *can be found in the text on page 50.)*
2. *Which of the features marked on the sketch-map are visible in the photograph of Sgurr Alasdair (square 4520)?*
3. *Which features of a typical large glaciated valley are found in Coir-uisg (around 4622)?*
4. *How easy would it be to walk around the coastline in this area? What obstacles would you encounter?*
5. *How many houses can you see on this map? Give reasons for the low density of population.*
6. *Describe the preparations you would need to make before attempting a ridge walk along the highest part of the Cuillin Hills.*

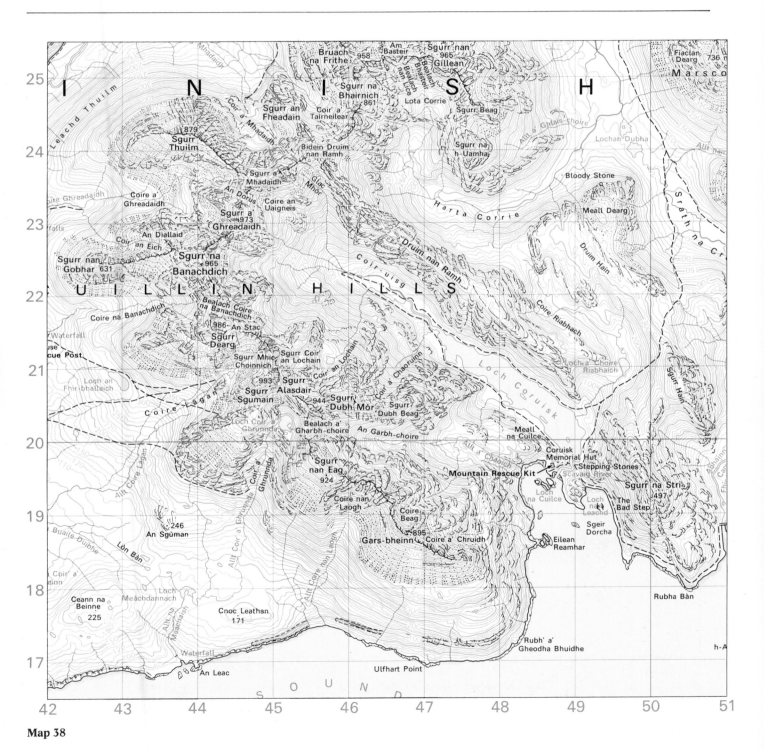

Map 38

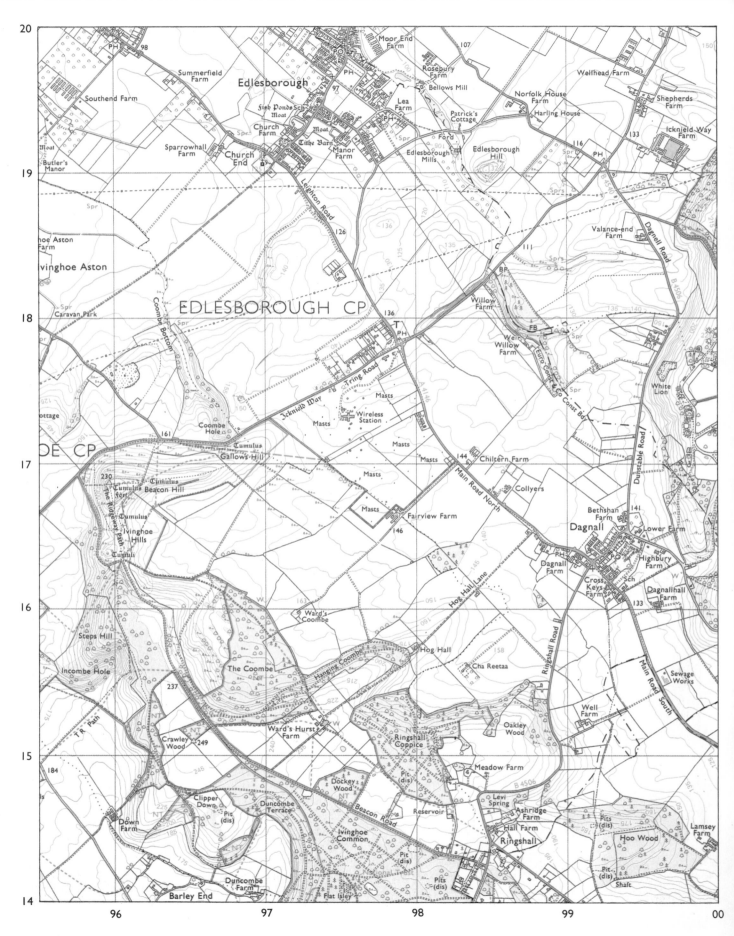

Map 39

First, a reminder that geographers tend to look for evidence about village sites, village shapes and village functions when they look at rural settlements on OS maps (see pages 18 to 21). In Section 1 we looked at a number of villages on 1:50 000 maps, so it is of interest to study here some contrasting villages on a 1:25 000 sheet. The area selected lies at the foot of the Chiltern Hills near Whipsnade Zoo. There are two lines of escarpments, one at Beacon Hill and one at the White Lion.

The famous White Lion cut in the chalk is visible for many kilometres around. Before tackling the exercise, it would be helpful to revise the importance of such technical terms as wet- and dry-point sites, permeable rocks, spring lines, and the features of an escarpment.

Exercise 36

1. (a) *Of the two villages of Edlesborough and Dagnall, which lies on clay, and which on chalk?*
   (b) *Which is a wet-point site using wells, and which a wet-point site using springs?*
2. *Contrast the size, shape and amenities of these two villages.*
3. *The earliest settlement in the area shown was on sites like Beacon Hill, many centuries before the Romans. Why were such sites chosen? What other evidence of pre-Roman settlement can you see on the map?*
4. (a) *Many people in this area live in dispersed settlements. Comment on the size, site and layout of the following farm communities:*
   Ward's Hurst Farm   9715

Chiltern Farm	*9817*
Willow Farm	*9817*
Summerfield Farm	*9619*
Southend Farm	*9519*
Icknield Way Farm	*9919*
Meadow Farm	*9814*

   (b) *Judging by the size of the fields, the height of the land, the angle of slope, and any land-use symbols (for orchards, rough pasture, etc.), try to give some sort of estimate of the size and speciality of at least three of the farms in (a).*
5. *Photo 38 shows Beacon Hill (9616) from the west. Make a sketch of this photograph and label as many features as you can from the map.*

Photo 38 *Ivinghoe Beacon, a hill-fort in Hertfordshire*

GROWTH OF A TOWN

Almost all of the large towns in Britain began as small settlements. Some started as villages, others as military centres. Over the centuries they have grown and spread over large areas of the surrounding countryside. Ordnance Survey maps often show the stages of growth in towns very clearly.

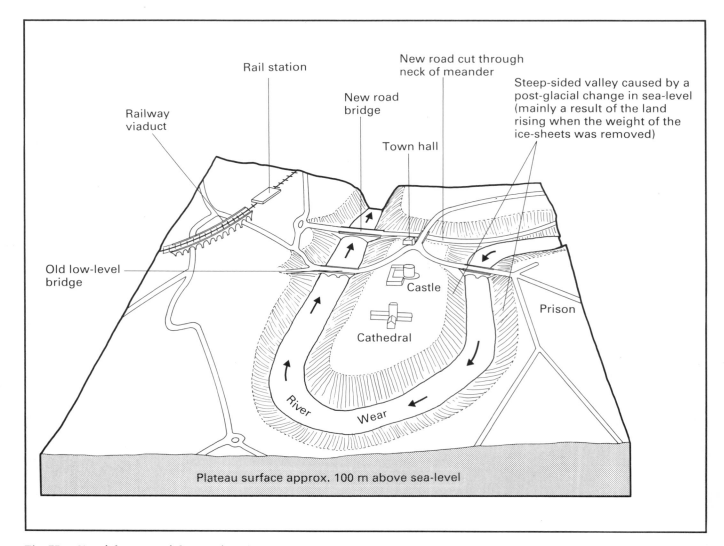

Fig. 57 *Site of the centre of the city of Durham*

Exercise 37

These questions concern the growth of Durham.

1. *What is the earliest settlement shown on the map of Durham (Map 40)? Approximately when was it built?*
2. *Durham's castle and cathedral, together with some of its older town houses and inns, date from between 1100 and 1700.*
   (a) *Explain why the castle was built in the precise location shown on the map.*
   (b) *Compare the site of Durham Castle with that of Warkworth Castle (page 20).*
   (c) *Both these castles stand on strategic sites within river-bends. Describe each site and how it was formed.*
3. *When the city grew during the eighteenth and nineteenth centuries it did not by any means spread out evenly from*
the historic core. How would you account for the distinctive growth-pattern of Durham between 1700 and 1920?
4. *Describe the view of Durham seen by rail travellers crossing the viaduct in square 2642 as shown in Photo 39.*
5. *The largest twentieth-century housing estates lie to the east of the city.*
   (a) *Name them.*
   (b) *Comment on their size, street layout and housing density compared with the older housing areas nearer to the centre.*
   (c) *How are housing and industry in the Gilesgate Moor area separated?*
6. *What sort of settlements are Sherburn (3142/3242) and Carrville (3043/3044)?*

Photo 39
Durham viewed from the railway

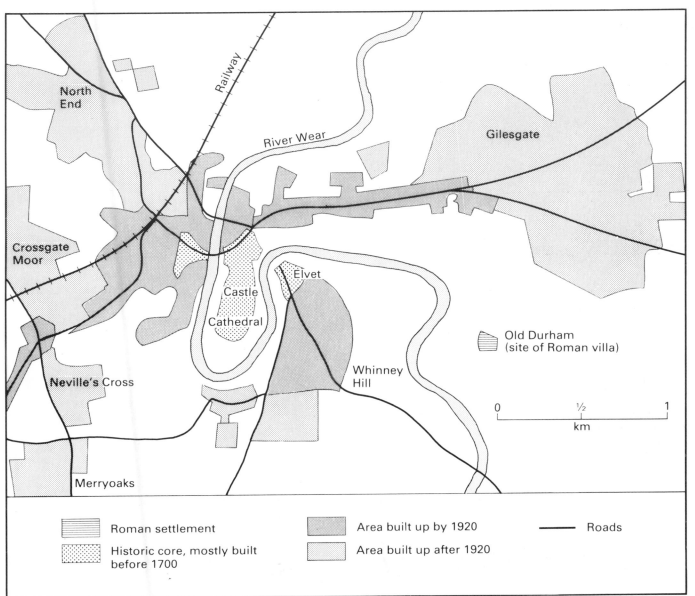

Fig. 58   *Stages of growth of the city of Durham*

Map 40

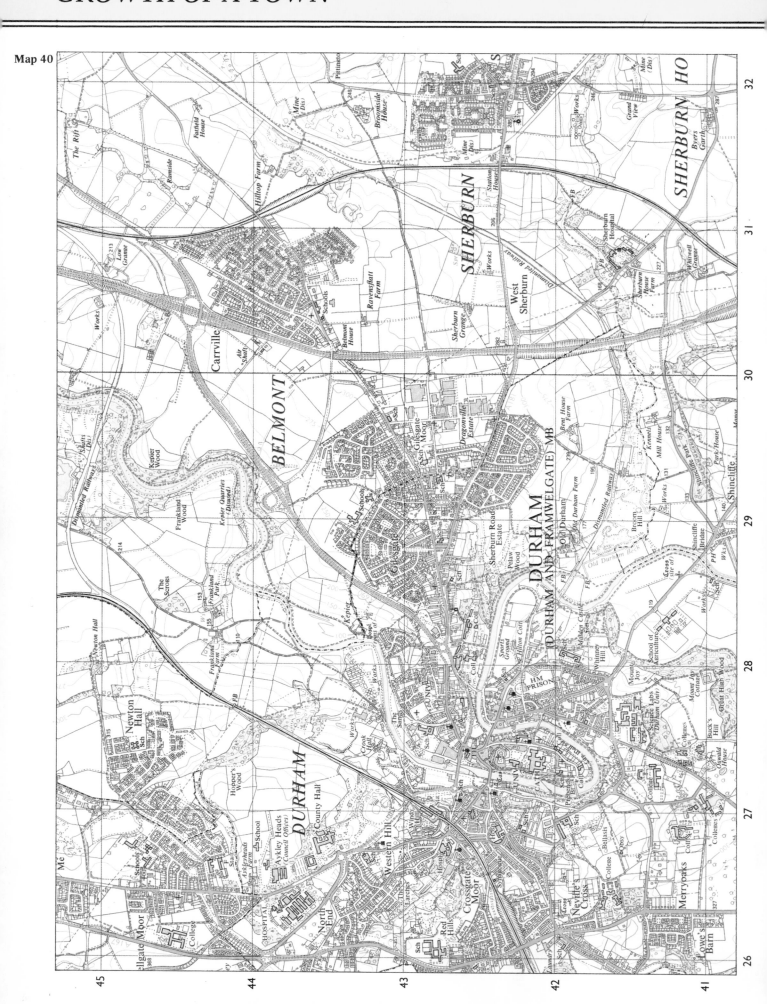

Photo 40   *Ancient buildings in Durham city centre*

Exercise 38

These questions are about planning and environmental issues in the Durham area, and relate to the resources on pages 56–59.

1. *Durham town centre is in a very restricted site, but it does have a certain 'old-world charm'. The problem is that shops don't have enough room to expand, and there is not enough car-parking space. As a result, many shoppers are abandoning Durham city and going either to the superstores in nearby Washington New Town or to the big stores of Newcastle-upon-Tyne. If you were a planner, what would you do about this problem?*

2. *Sherburn is an example of a mining community whose pit has closed.*
   (a) *Give the grid reference of the old mine.*
   (b) *How do communities try to adapt to these changes?*
   (c) *Where might former miners look for new jobs within the area of the map?*

3. (a) *Make a sketch-map to show what the railway network on this map would have looked like when all the lines were in operation.*
   (b) *Why have so many lines closed?*
   (c) *What are some of the social consequences of this?*

4. *Imagine that you lived in the house in the Carrville estate where grid lines 31 and 44 cross. Where might you go for*

   (a) *local shopping?*
   (b) *a pleasant walk, not far from home?*
   (c) *an evening class at a college?*
   (d) *an operation (in a large hospital)?*
   (e) *lodging a complaint about a local planning issue?*
   (f) *playing some kind of sport?*

5. (a) *Would your outer-suburban house be conveniently placed for the activities in question 4?*
   (b) *Where in Durham might you move to in order to be closer to the major amenities of the city?*

6. *If you were hoping to buy a house in Durham, where might you expect to find*
   (a) *cheap houses?*
   (b) *moderately priced houses?*
   (c) *expensive houses (within the city)?*

7. (a) *If you were in charge of a large group of stores selling self-assembly furniture, where in Durham would you consider opening up a branch? (Remember that you would need plenty of space for a large show-room, a warehouse and car-parking.)*
   (b) *How might your new store challenge traders with shops in the centre of Durham?*

8. *Central Durham is also shown on a 1:50 000 scale map on page 68 (Map 45). Compare the information available on this map with the data on Map 40 (1:25 000 scale).*

NEW TOWNS

We have seen how most towns and cities have developed over many centuries and have distinctive growth-patterns. Obviously, these towns have expanded bit by bit, for although particular roads and estates may have been carefully planned, there would not have been any fixed overall design for the town as a whole. In contrast, new towns develop in a highly organized way. Before building starts, a **master plan** is drawn up and approved. Each phase of growth of the new town has to agree with this plan.

Master plans of new towns usually include a *civic centre*; neighbourhood *housing areas* with their own shops, schools, community centres, etc.; *industrial estates*; planned *open space*, and a pattern of *major roads* to link each zone of the town.

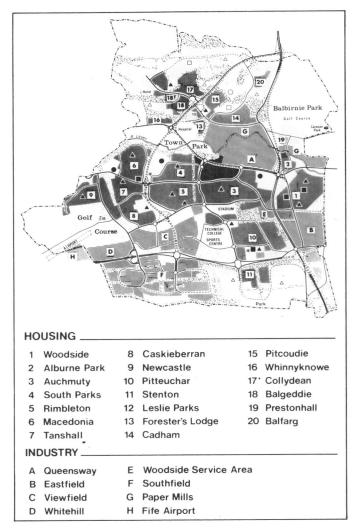

Exercise 39

1. *Using Map 41 and the resources on this page, give six-figure map references for a point in each of the following areas of Glenrothes:*
   (a) *the commercial centre*
   (b) *an industrial estate*
   (c) *a neighbourhood housing area*
   (d) *a large area of planned open space.*
2. (a) *Which parts of Glenrothes have yet to be built?*
   (b) *What does the master plan suggest that these areas will eventually be used for?*
3. *Judging from the map evidence shown here, why should a new town be needed in this part of Scotland?*
4. *Write a detailed report contrasting the layout of roads, housing types, industries, open spaces and amenities in Kirkcaldy and Glenrothes.*

HOUSING

1	Woodside	8	Caskieberran	15	Pitcoudie
2	Alburne Park	9	Newcastle	16	Whinnyknowe
3	Auchmuty	10	Pitteuchar	17	Collydean
4	South Parks	11	Stenton	18	Balgeddie
5	Rimbleton	12	Leslie Parks	19	Prestonhall
6	Macedonia	13	Forester's Lodge	20	Balfarg
7	Tanshall	14	Cadham		

INDUSTRY

A	Queensway	E	Woodside Service Area
B	Eastfield	F	Southfield
C	Viewfield	G	Paper Mills
D	Whitehill	H	Fife Airport

Fig. 59   *Master plan of Glenrothes New Town*

Photo 41   *Glenrothes from the air*

HINTERLANDS AND SERVICE AREAS

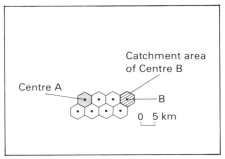

Fig. 60.1 *Low-order service catchment areas. People living in the area marked* ▢ *will shop at centre A, people living in the area marked* ▨ *will shop at centre B, and so on, when buying everyday goods such as bread and newspapers.*

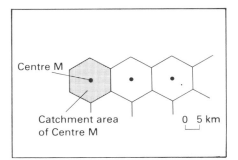

Fig. 60.2 *Medium-order service catchment areas. For more specialized services, such as entertainment, schools, banks, buying clothes and hardware, people will travel further, to a larger centre (M).*

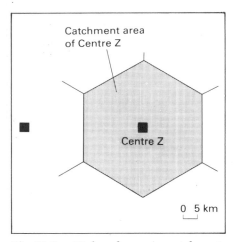

Fig. 60.3 *High-order service catchment areas. For very specialized services, such as a theatre, a further education college or a large department store, people will travel long distances to a major regional centre (Z).*

As we saw on pages 22 and 23, the distance that people are prepared to travel in order to buy something is proportional to how expensive and how specialized that item is. Nobody would make a 30-kilometre round trip to buy a packet of fruit gums, but such a journey would be worth making to save £50 on a set of chairs. In any region there tend to be a lot of small settlements with only basic services (such as a grocer's shop), a moderate number of medium-sized centres with a wider range of services (like banks, secondary schools and hospitals) and a few very large regional centres providing almost all major services (such as a university, an international airport and a stock exchange).

How far people are prepared to travel to purchase an item or a service is called *the range of a good*. A 'league table' that shows a lot of small centres, a moderate number of intermediate centres, a few large centres, and just one capital (or *primate*) city is called a *hierarchy*. If towns are listed in order of their number of inhabitants, the biggest will generally have the highest *rank*, and the smallest the lowest rank, though there are some fascinating exceptions.

The area from which people are prepared to travel regularly into a centre for a service is called a *catchment area* and operates much like river catchment areas (see page 40). The minimum number of people needed for a service, such as a cinema, to operate is called the *threshold population*.

Exercise 40

Use all the data on this and the following page to help you answer these questions.
1. *If you were setting up a firm to distribute bread to baker's shops in the area shown in Map 42, where would you locate your depot?*
2. *Why do so many major roads radiate from Aberdeen?*
3. *What is the average distance between market towns in the lowland area (the scale of the map is 1:625 000, or about 10 miles to 1 inch)?*
4. *Why may small settlements in the mountain area in the south-west of the map have more services than settlements of equivalent size near Aberdeen?*
5. *Why are the catchment areas for middle-order services in this part of north-east Scotland not all the same size and shape? (You may like to try to explain the odd shapes of some of the catchment areas.)*
6. *Using an atlas, find out which neighbouring centres are likely to offer the same extensive range of services as Aberdeen, and which will therefore be of equivalent rank.*
7. *Imagine that you lived in Rhynie (14 kilometres south of Huntly). Where would you go to obtain the following goods and services?*
   (a) A packet of fruit gums
   (b) A week's groceries
   (c) A secondary school
   (d) Fashionable clothes
   (e) An international airport
8. *Aberdeen has grown rapidly since the development of North Sea oil. The catchment area now extends far out into the North Sea to include the oil rigs. List those services which you think will have developed as a result of this increased catchment area.*

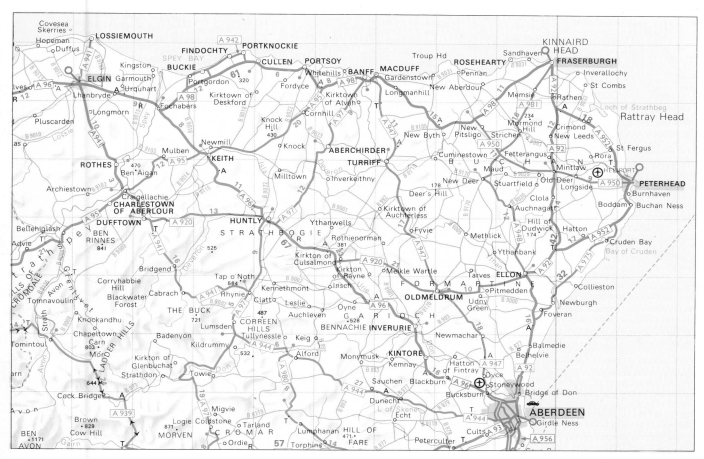

Map 42

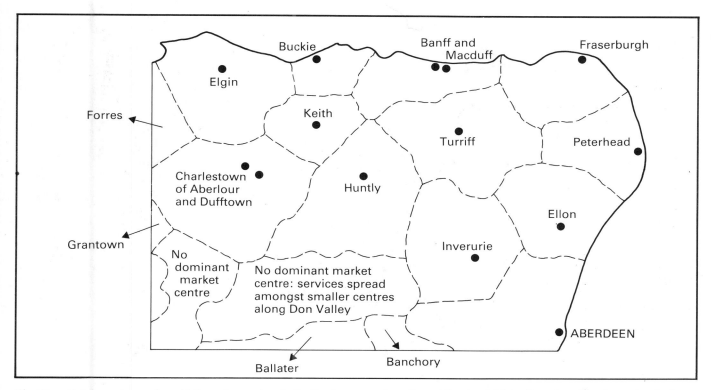

Fig. 61 *Catchment areas for middle-order services in the Buchan area of north-east Scotland. Elgin, Fraserburgh and Peterhead all have a greater range of services and may be considered as major market centres serving part of the region. Aberdeen is a regional centre for the whole of the area shown on this map, providing a full range of specialized services.*

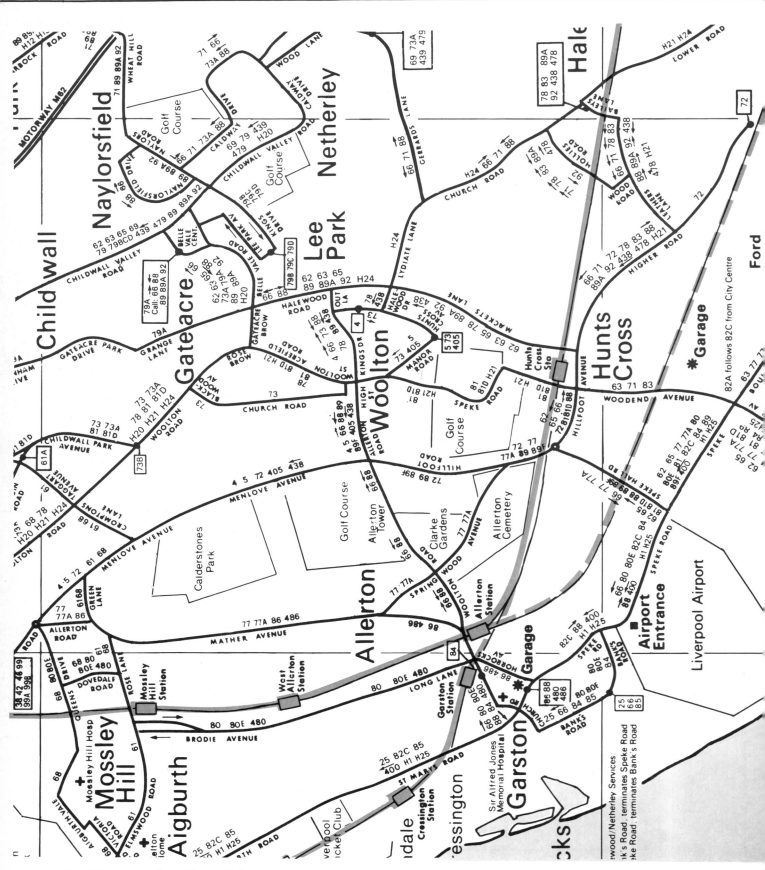

Map 43   *Extract from Merseyside bus map.*

'Life skills' are the sorts of things we must be able to do easily and efficiently if we are to cope with the everyday demands of modern living. One such skill is knowing how to move around a city by public transport. This seems to baffle a lot of people, young and old. They usually give up and ask passers-by for help. How well could you tackle the tasks set in Exercise 41?

Exercise 41

1. *You have been invited to visit someone you met on holiday. Your friend's house is at the junction of Rose Brow and Gateacre Brow in Gateacre, near Liverpool. You are arriving by inter-city train at Lime Street Station. Your friend advises you to catch a local train to Allerton Station, and then get two buses.*
   (a) *Which local railway line do you take?*
   (b) *Which bus routes will you use?*
   (c) *Where must you change buses?*
2. *A family living in West Kirkby, on the Wirral, have booked a holiday in Spain. The plane flies from Liverpool Airport. To save on airport car-park charges, they decide to go by public transport.*
   (a) *Use Map 43 to name the railway station nearest to the airport.*
   (b) *Which railway lines would they use? Where would they change trains? (See Fig. 62.)*
   (c) *Which bus would they catch to the airport entrance?*

Photo 42   *Bus maps can be related to route-indicators on buses and route-numbers on bus-stops.*

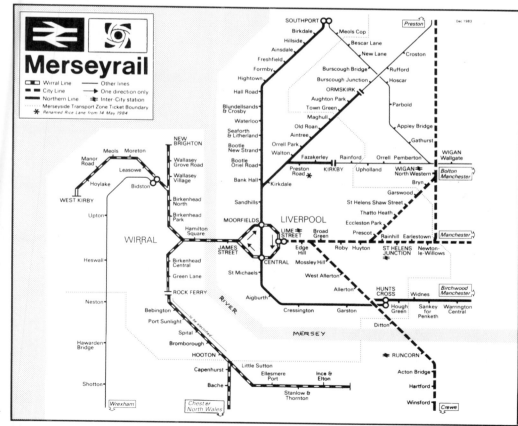

Fig. 62   *Part of the Merseyrail network*

Nothing upsets the start of a car journey more than arguments about which way to go: 'Let's go the pretty way', 'Let's go the fastest way', 'Let's avoid the big traffic jams', 'Let's keep away from the towns' and so on. Even when the route is agreed in advance difficulties may arise when people follow road signs rather than their maps, or miss turnings and don't bother to backtrack. Time, tempers and fuel are needlessly used up because motorists don't use their maps well. Good navigation is a skill every driver should develop.

Exercise 42

1. *'Come into Denbigh on the A541. Take the B-road out of town and follow it right over the hills, past the Brenig Reservoir. At Cerrigydrudion, go along the Corwen road for a while before branching right on a B-road again. This will eventually take you to Bala. Then all you have to do is cross the bridge at the end of the lake and drive alongside the lake to the hotel at Llangower.'*

   Armed with this information (provided by the hotel), follow the route on Map 44 and draw a simple sketch-map to stick to your car dashboard. Add any extra details that would be helpful.

2. *The rough map (Fig. 63) shows a round trip from Llandudno you and your family planned over breakfast. Imagine that you are going to be navigating.*
   (a) *Using Map 44, give directions and road numbers for each leg of the route.*
   (b) *The scale of the map is 1:250 000. The grid lines are 10 kilometres apart. Estimate the approximate length of the round trip to the nearest 10 kilometres.*
   (c) *If you drive at an average speed of 50 k.p.h., how many hours will the journey take?*

3. *What is the shortest route from Denbigh to Llanrwst? (The scale is 1:250 000, or 1 centimetre to 2.5 kilometres.) Give the numbers of the roads used and the total distance.*

4. *You have to go from Prestatyn to Conwy on a bank holiday Monday. There is a carnival at Colwyn Bay and a series of major roadworks in Abergele. Find a reasonably direct inland route that will avoid the traffic jams on the coast roads. Give the numbers of the roads you use and the names of major places you pass through.*

Photo 44   *In Wales, the most direct route isn't always the quickest!*

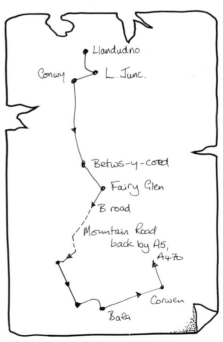

Fig. 63

Map 44

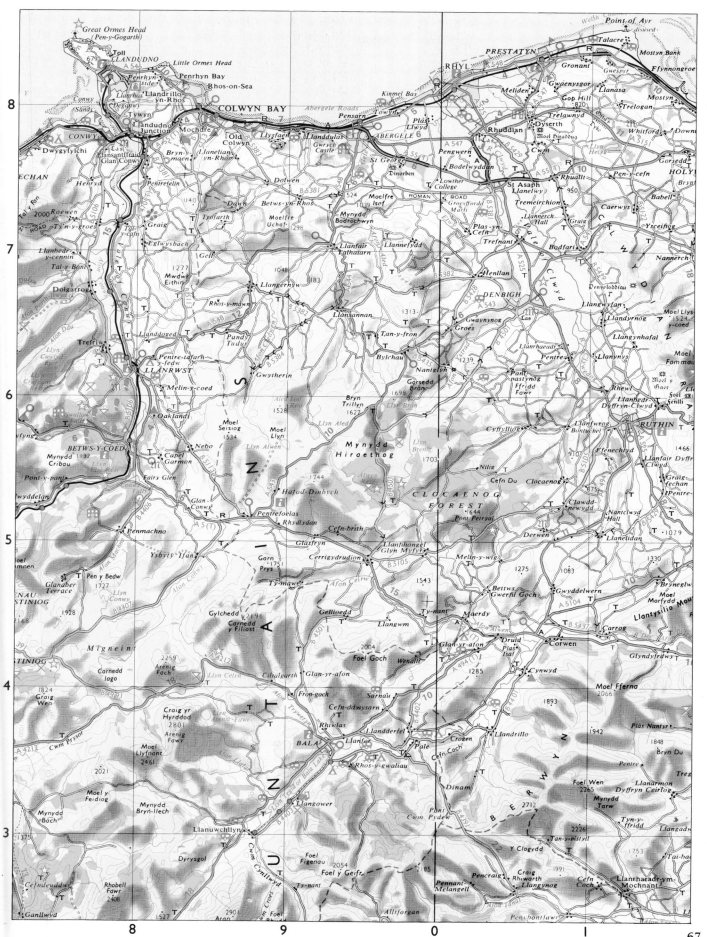

PLANNING A RAIL JOURNEY

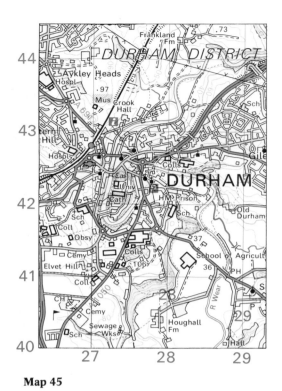

Map 45

Travel by rail involves not only reading timetables and making connections, but getting to and from stations. Imagine you are going from the science laboratories in Durham University (Map 45: 276415) to Liverpool University (Map 46: 362902). You are to travel by inter-city trains from Durham Station to Lime Street, Liverpool. You will need to change trains at two points along the journey.

Exercise 43

1. *The most appropriate schedule for the railway journey from Durham to Liverpool is shown in Fig. 65.*
   (a) If you were to walk from Durham University science laboratories to Durham station, which would be the shortest route? (Refer to Map 45 or Map 40, page 58.)
   (b) How far is it?
   (c) How long would it take you if you walked at 5 k.p.h.?
   (d) At what time should you set off to give yourself long enough to reach the station and buy a ticket for the 10.25 train?

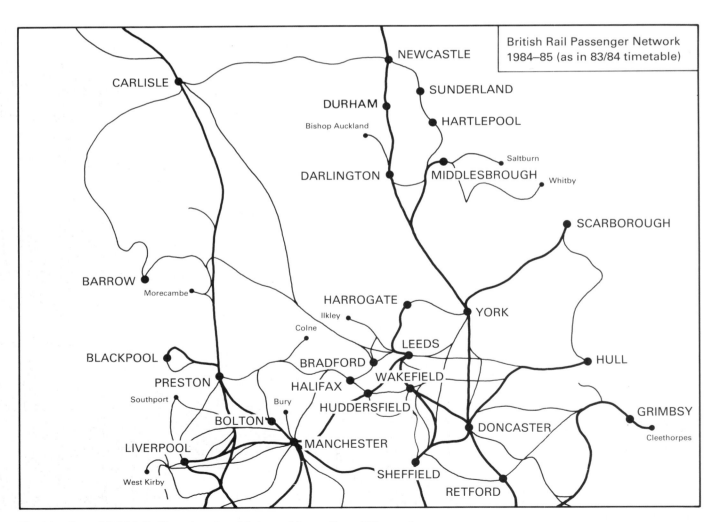

Fig. 64 *Part of British Rail's route network between Newcastle and Liverpool*

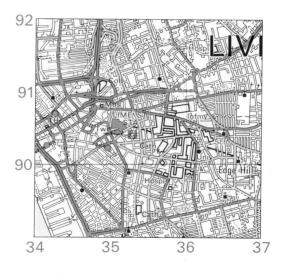

Map 46

Exercise 44

1. You have got into the 10.25 train at Durham.
   (a) Where will you first change trains?
   (b) At which stations will you stop before you change trains?
   (c) When will you arrive in Liverpool?
2. Which local stations will you pass through between St Helens and Lime Street? (See Fig. 62, page 65.)
3. As you come out of Lime Street Station, what landmarks would you see around you? (See Map 46.)
4. (a) Map 46 shows which district of Liverpool the university is in. Give its name.
   (b) If you used Merseyrail (see Fig. 62, page 65) to get to the university, on which line would you travel?

Exercise 45

Suppose that, instead of using Merseyrail, you decided to use a taxi to get from Lime Street Station to the university. If a taxi costs 60p per mile, plus a fixed charge of £1, plus a tip of 25p, how much would the taxi-ride cost you altogether?

26 Newcastle	..	..	.. d	10 10
26 Durham			.. d	10 25
26 Darlington	..	..	.. d	10 43
York		34 d		11 54
Ulleskelf	..	..	34 d	....
Church Fenton		34 d		....
Micklefield			d	....
Garforth	..	..	d	....
Cross Gates			d	....
Leeds	..	..	a	12 24
Leeds		40 d		12 26
Bramley..	..	.. † 40 d		....
New Pudsey		40 d		....
Bradford Interchange	..	40 a		....
			d	....
Halifax	..	..	d	....
Sowerby Bridge			d	....
Mytholmroyd	..	..	d	....
Hebden Bridge			d	....
Todmorden	..	..	d	....
Littleborough			d	....
Rochdale		93 d		....
Castleton	..	..	d	....
Moston ..	..	..	d	....
Morley			d	....
Batley	..	..	.. d	....
Dewsbury			d	12 41
Ravensthorpe	..	..	d	....
Mirfield		33 d		....
Deighton		33 d		....
Huddersfield		33 a		12 51
			d	12 53
Slaithwaite			d	....
Marsden ...	..	..	d	....
Greenfield			d	....
Mossley	..	..	d	....
Stalybridge			d	13 16
Ashton-under-Lyne			d	....
Park	..	..	.. d	....
Miles Platting		93 d		13 32
Manchester Victoria	..	93 a		13 32
St. Helens Junction		99 a		14 18
Liverpool Lime Street	..	99 a		14 45

Fig. 65 *Part of the British Rail timetable for trains between York and Manchester, with connections from Newcastle and to Liverpool*

Photo 45 *Taxis outside Lime Street Station, Liverpool*

CHOOSING THE BEST ROUTE

Get a group of motorists together and before long they will be discussing the best route from one place to another. Some people favour the most direct route. Others will add great distances to their journeys in order to stay on the motorways. What matters to many is not so much the distance between A and B as the time it takes.

Exercise 46 gives you a simulated car-journey from Nottingham to Basingstoke. For the sake of realism five alternative routes are suggested. You will have to take into account both time and distance when you decide which route is best. To make measurements use Map 47, which is a route-planning map drawn to the scale of 1:1 375 000 (approximately 1 inch to 22 miles). The exercise would be best conducted in miles, as at present British road distances are generally given in miles rather than kilometres

and most people talk in terms of m.p.h., not k.p.h.

When you complete the chart in Exercise 46, take into account the following average speeds (they allow for stops and delays):

Motorways (shown in *blue*): 60 m.p.h., or 1.0 miles per minute.
Primary routes (shown in *green*): 45 m.p.h., or 0.75 miles per minute.
Other main roads (shown in *red*): 30 m.p.h., or 0.5 miles per minute.

Note: 60 miles equals roughly 100 kilometres.

Add 10 minutes to your journey every time you go through a town (marked with a black circle) and 20 minutes for a city (marked with a black square). If you go into London, add an hour for congestion.

Exercise 46

1. Complete this chart with the information provided.

Route	Roads used	Approximate distance in miles			Total distance in miles	Total time*
		Motorways	Primary routes	Other roads		
A	M1–M69–A423–A34–A339					
B	M1 to edge of London–London Ring Road–A316–M3					
C	M1–A43–A34–A339					
D	M1–A43–A413 to Amersham–High Wycombe–Maidenhead–M4–A33					
E†	M1 to Watford–Slough–M4–A33					

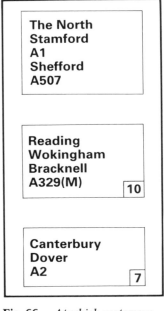

The North
Stamford
A1
Shefford
A507

Reading
Wokingham
Bracknell
A329(M) 10

Canterbury
Dover
A2 7

Fig. 66 *At which motorway junctions on Map 47 would you see these signs?*

Notes: *Don't forget to include ten minutes' delay for each town you go through.*
†*In Route E, the primary road link between Watford and Slough will be replaced by the M25 Motorway after 1986.*

2. *Which of the above routes would you select for:*
  (a) someone in a hurry, like a sales representative,
  (b) a holiday-maker bored with too much motorway driving,
  (c) someone who is keen to save petrol, and who keeps the car mileage down to the minimum possible?

3. *(a) Trace the motorway network shown in Map 47.*
  (b) Join up the existing parts of the M25 to make a

complete ring around London, and complete the M3 to Winchester.
  (c) Now assume that you were a government minister with enough money to finance the construction of a further 100 miles (160 kilometres) of motorways in the area covered by Map 47. Where would you build these motorways, and why?

SHEFFIELD Rotherham Bawtry Gainsborough Market Rasen Louth Mablethorpe
Worksop A1 Lincoln Horncastle Skegness
Chesterfield Mansfield Newark-on-Trent Sleaford Boston Hunstanton Wells-next-the-Sea Cromer
Matlock Ripley Nottingham Grantham Spalding King's Lynn THE WASH Fakenham North Walsham
Ashbourne Derby Loughborough Melton Mowbray Wisbech Downham Market East Dereham Swaffham Norwich Caist
Ashby-de-la-Zouch Oakham Stamford Peterborough March Wymondham Acle Gre Yar
Tamworth Leicester Corby Oundle Chatteris Ely Thetford Diss Bungay Beccles Lo
Nuneaton Hinckley Market Harborough Thrapston Huntingdon Newmarket Bury St Edmunds Saxmundham
COVENTRY Rugby Kettering Wellingborough St Neots Cambridge Stowmarket Ipswich Aldeburgh
Royal Leamington Spa Warwick Northampton Bedford Royston Haverhill Sudbury Felixstowe Harwich Orford Ness
Stratford-upon-Avon Daventry Towcester Stevenage Great Dunmow Halstead Braintree Colchester The Naze
Banbury Brackley Milton Keynes Buckingham Bicester Dunstable Luton Bishop's Stortford Harlow Chelmsford Clacton-on-Sea
Chipping Norton Woodstock Aylesbury St Albans Hertford Potters Bar Epping Brentwood
Witney Oxford Thame High Wycombe Watford Amersham LONDON Basildon Southend-on-Sea
Abingdon Henley-on-Thames Maidenhead Slough Tilbury Gravesend Sheerness Herne Bay Margate
Swindon Wantage Reading Heathrow Airport Dartford Chatham Sittingbourne Ramsgate North Forela
Hungerford Newbury Wokingham Camberley Croydon Orpington Maidstone Canterbury Sandwich Deal The Downs
Marlborough Basingstoke Guildford Dorking Woking Esher Reigate Sevenoaks Royal Tunbridge Wells Ashford Dover South Foreland
Andover Farnham Gatwick Airport East Grinstead Tenterden Folkestone
Stockbridge Alton Godalming Crawley Heathfield New Romney STRAIT OF DOVER
Winchester Romsey Haslemere Billingshurst Horsham Haywards Heath Rye Lydd Dungeness
Petersfield Midhurst Hailsham Hastings
Southampton Fareham Arundel Worthing Lewes Bexhill
Ringwood Chichester Brighton Newhaven Eastbourne Beachy Head
Lymington Portsmouth Bognor Regis Selsey Bill
Cowes Ryde
The Needles Yarmouth ISLE OF WIGHT Ventnor St Catherine's Point

Scale 1:1,375,000

| Miles 20 | | 0 | | 20 | | 40 | | 60 |
| Kilometres | 20 | 0 | 20 | 40 | 60 | 80 | 100 |

MOTORWAY DIVERSION

'Travel newsflash . . . The M6 motorway has been closed between Junctions 25 and 27 in both directions because of a serious accident at Orrell.'

This news reaches you on the car radio as you approach Junction 24 from the south. The police are turning all northbound traffic off the motorway on to the A49 at Junction 25.

Decide which route you are going to take from the M6 link/A49 junction (568020) to Junction 27 (543106), where you can continue your journey northwards to Preston. Bear in mind the following:

● It will take you these times to cross a 1-kilometre square from south to north:
  Dual carriageway: 1 minute
  'A' road in rural (country) surroundings: 2 minutes
  'A' road in urban (town) surroundings: 5 minutes
  'B' road: 3 minutes (rural), 6 minutes (urban)
  Unclassified road: 4 minutes (rural), 8 minutes (urban)

● If you go under the railway bridge at 567046 you must expect a four-minute delay because of bridge repairs.

● The official diversion is: A49 to Newtown, along the minor road (squares 5605 and 5606) to the B5375, west on the B5375 to Shevington, north on the B5206 to Junction 27. This is very congested and traffic is slow-moving.

Exercise 47

1. *The official diversion would take you 42 minutes. If the motorway was open, it would only take six minutes between Junctions 25 and 27. How late will you be if you take the official diversion?*
2. *Work out another route between Junctions 25 and 27.*
   (a) *Draw a sketch-map that you can refer to while driving along that route.*
   (b) *Calculate how many minutes late you would be if you followed your route.*
3. *Notice how the M6, like all motorways, avoids town centres. The old road north was the A49. Follow the A49 north-south on this map and describe how different long-distance travel was before motorways were built.*

Photo 46 *Traffic congestion in Wigan*

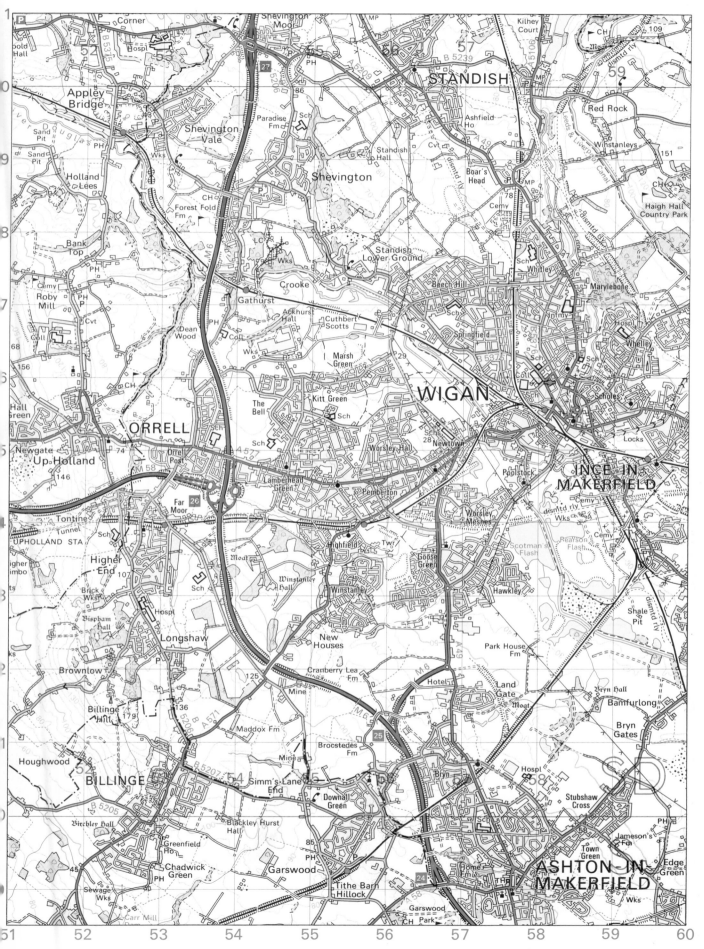

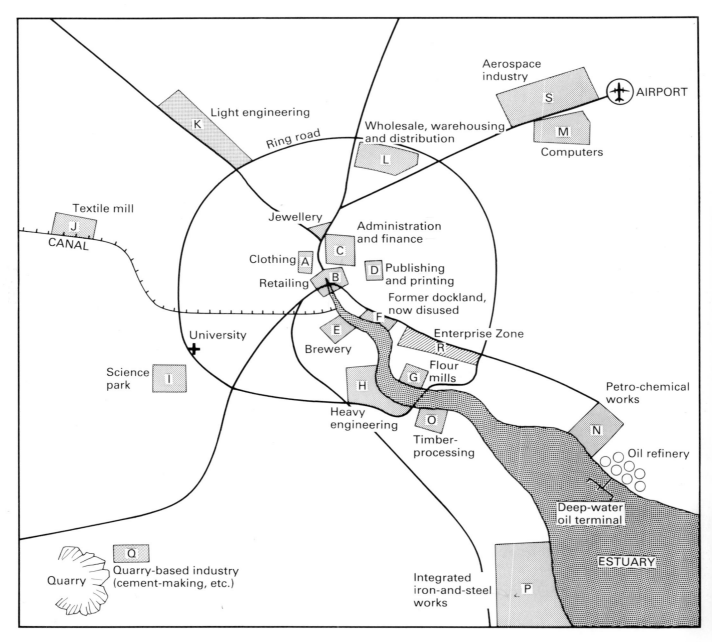

Fig. 67 *This sketch-map shows the likely location of a number of typical industries in an imaginary town in Britain. The industries are labelled A to S.*

Exercise 48

1. *Complete the last column of this chart.*

Description	Letters on the map
Old, decaying Victorian industrial activity	
Industry sited close to raw materials	
Industry sited in or near the city CBD	
Port-based industry	
Modern 'high-tech' industry	
Industry deliberately sited close to major road routes	

2. *Find examples of as many of the types of industry in Fig. 67 as you can on Map 57 (page 87). A sketch-map showing the Mersey estuary and the major roads and railway lines would help you to record these locations.*

3. *Which types of industries offer the best prospects for new jobs? If you were looking for a house in the Liverpool area, where might you choose to live to be near to your most likely workplace?*

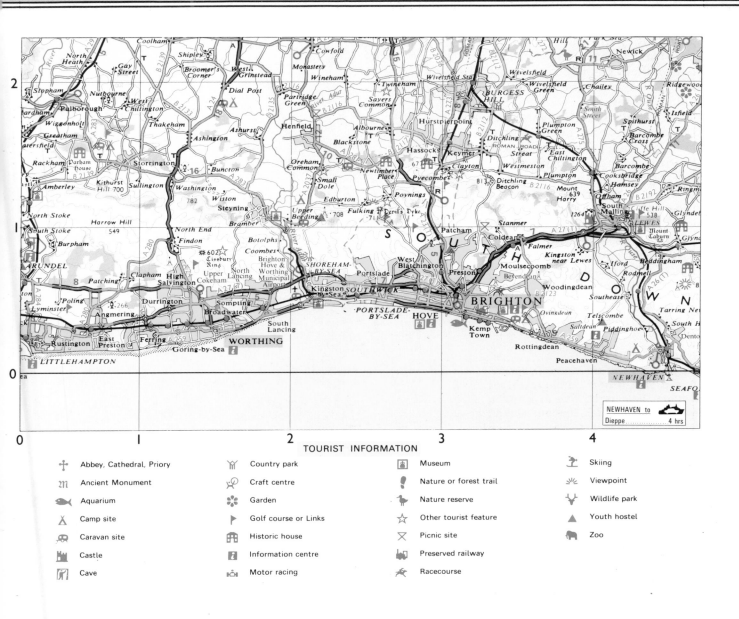

Map 49

Exercise 49

Imagine that you have decided to have a week's holiday in a hotel in Worthing. Here is the schedule you have planned:

Day 1: *A day at the horse-races, travelling by train*

Day 2: *Train journey to a neighbouring town that offers plenty of interest*

Day 3: *Rent a car to visit three historic houses and a museum, stopping for a picnic lunch*

Day 4: *Visit to another seaside resort not yet visited*

Day 5: *A second day using trains, travelling in a different direction to that on Day 2*

Day 6: *Rent a car to visit some of the scenic viewpoints in the area*

Day 7: *A game of golf near the coast*

Using the 1: 250 000 (1 cm to 2.5 km) map with tourist features (Map 49, above), plan these seven days in more detail.

For many years bus companies have tried to encourage walkers to use their country services to reach pleasant rural areas for hiking. Buses give walkers one distinct advantage over car-drivers: you can do a single-direction walk without having to return to where you parked your car. However, there are also problems. Country buses run infrequently and if you fail to catch your planned connection you could be in for a long wait!

See how you get on planning one of the bus-assisted country walks suggested in Exercise 50.

Exercise 50

Imagine that you are staying in Bristol. It is a fine, warm Saturday in the summer. You would like to go for a walk in the country, but you haven't got a car. After checking at the bus station you decide that it would be pleasant to explore the area around Blagdon Lake (shown in Map 50).

Look at Fig. 68. It is a page from the Bristol area bus-timetable for services 373, 374 and 375. If you assume that you can walk across a 1-km grid square in approximately 20 minutes, and that you intend to stop at a pub around lunch-time, how might you use the map and timetable to plan your day? (Note: Winford is in the north-east corner of the map, around 540650.)

Suggested Walks:
- *Winford to Blagdon via Butcombe*
- *Ubley to Blagdon via Butcombe*
- *Blagdon to Winford via Nempnett Thrubwell*
- *Ubley to Ubley around the lake*

Write your route in 'legs', like this ▶

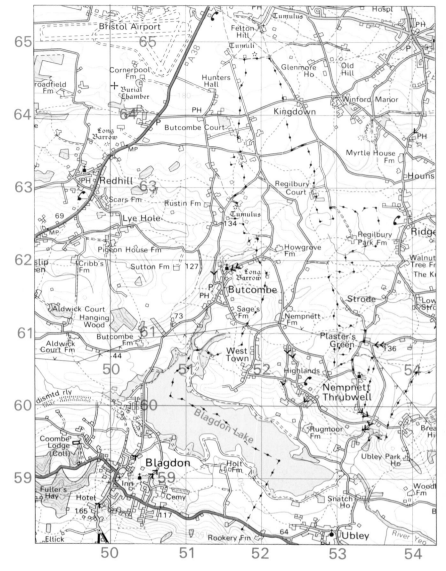

Map 50

From	To	Route	Distance	Time taken
Bristol	Ubley	Bus № 374	—	1 hour 28 mins
Ubley	Inn at Blagdon	footpath	3 km	1 hour
—	—	lunch at Inn	—	1 hour

Fig. 68 *Timetable for bus services in the Bristol area*

Mondays to Saturdays ✱

Service No.	375 S	374	374 NS	374 NS	373 NS	375
BRISTOL, Bus Station	0630	0840	1420	1420	1625‡	1745†
Whitchurch, Black Lion	0648	....	....	....	....	1803
Pensford Hill (Top)	0655	....	....	....	....	1810
Stanton Drew, Round House	0700	....	....	....	....	1815
Dundry Church	....	....	....	....	1652	....
Dundry Chapel	....	....	....	....	1655	....
Barrow Gurney, Fountain	....	0902	1442	1442	....	....
Winford Hospital	....	....	1447	1447	....	....
Winford, Prince of Waterloo	....	0908	1451	1451	....	....
Chew Stoke, Pilgrims' Way Cross Roads	....	0917	1500	1500	1706	....
Chew Magna, Post Office	0704	0921	1504	1504	1710	1819
Chew Stoke Inn	0709	....	....	....	....	1824
Bishop Sutton, Red Lion	0717	0933	1516	1516	1722	1832
West Harptree, Crown	0725	0941	1533■	1524	1730	1840
East Harptree, Clock	....	....	1537	1528	....	1844
West Harptree, Crown	....	0941	1541	1532	1730	1848
Compton Martin	....	0944	1544	1535	1733	1851
Ubley, Saw Mills	....	0948	1548	1539	1737	1855
BLAGDON, Seymour Arms	....	0955	1555	1546	1744	1902
Burrington Turn	....	....	....	....	1749	1907
Langford Court	....	....	....	....	1753	1911

Service No.	375 NS	375 S	373 NS	374	374
Langford Court	0659	....	0834	....	....
Burrington Turn	0703	....	0838	....	....
BLAGDON, Seymour Arms	0708	....	0843	1000	1803
Ubley, Saw Mills	0715	....	0850	1007	1610
Compton Martin	0719	....	0854	1011	1614
West Harptree, Crown	0722	....	0857	1014	1617
East Harptree, Clock	0726	....	0901	1018	....
West Harptree, Crown	0730	0730	0905	1022	1617
Bishop Sutton, Red Lion	0738	0738	0913	1030	1625
Chew Stoke Inn	0746	0746	....	....	....
Chew Magna, Post Office	0751	0751	0925	1042	1637
Chew Stoke, Pilgrims' Way Cross Roads	....	....	0929	1046	....
Winford, Prince of Waterloo	....	....	1055	1646	
Winford Hospital	....	....	....	....	1650
Barrow Gurney, Fountain	....	....	....	1101	1655
Dundry Chapel	....	....	0940	....	....
Dundry Church	....	....	0943	....	....
Stanton Drew, Round House	0755	0755	....	....	....
Pensford Hill (Top)	0800	0800	....	....	....
Whitchurch, Black Lion	0807	0807	....	....	....
BRISTOL, Bus Station	0825	0825	1010	1123	1717

CODE

✱ — Not Bank Holiday Mondays, Good Friday or Boxing Day.
■ — Arrives 1524.
† — The first setting-down point on this journey on Mondays to Fridays is Whitchurch.

‡ — The first setting-down point on this journey is Bridgwater Road (Kings Head).
NS— Not Saturdays.
S— Saturdays only.

If you plan to walk not along leafy country lanes and footpaths (as in Map 50) but on high, remote, rugged uplands (as in Map 51), the ability to use an OS map changes from a useful skill into an essential, life-saving skill. If you cannot read contour patterns, you may plan a route that turns out to be beyond your ability to complete. If you cannot measure distances, you could again be in trouble. If the mist comes down when you are on high ground without a compass, and you cannot find the direction to your destination, you may be dangerously lost.

As we discovered from Map 38, the hills on the Isle of Skye are remote, steep and challenging. Western Scotland is often subject to rapid changes in weather, especially when a north-westerly wind is blowing. Yet it is worth overcoming these difficulties to enjoy the beautiful scenery, provided that you plan your expeditions with care and don't take risks.

Imagine that you are staying at the youth hostel in Glen Brittle (square 4022). After an evening meal you sit around the table with your friends to plan the next day's journey. You intend to cross the uplands of Glen Brittle Forest to reach Eynort. Which of the routes in Fig. 69 would you most favour, and why?

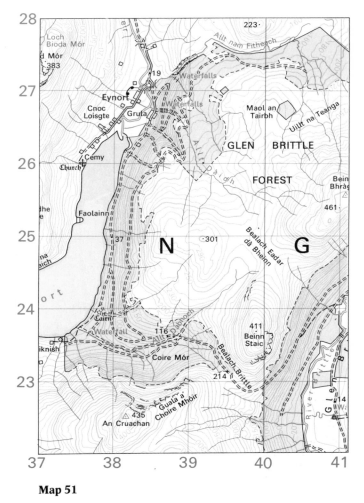

Map 51

Exercise 51

1. *If you are to walk safely in hills like the ones shown in Map 51, what items of clothing and safety equipment must you take with you?*
2. *Imagine that you have opted for Route B. You reached the source of the stream at 403247 about 15 minutes' walking time ago. Suddenly the cloud-level falls and you are shrouded in swirling hill mist.*
   (a) *Where do you think you are? (How fast do you walk? How steep was the gradient? What clues did you observe?)*
   (b) *Approximately what compass bearing should you follow to aim for the bridge at 384271?*
   (c) *What landmarks would you look out for as you follow this bearing to confirm your location?*
   (d) *How far do you need to travel?*
3. *As it turns out, the cloud-base is 200 metres above sea-level. You find out that you were exactly on course. Where will you be when you drop below the cloud-base?*

Fig. 69 *Route A is a safe route, following forest tracks. It is indirect, however, and seldom breaks out into open ground.*
Route B involves climbing a steep gully before crossing the Bealach Eadar da Bheinn watershed. Descent is by the Allt Dàidh valley. It would be easy to get lost in the featureless watershed area.
Route C is certainly direct, but tackling the cliff-face of Beinn Staic would require rock-climbing skills. This is the shortest but most difficult route, only for those who are fit and well equipped.
Route D involves ascending to 461 metres via a gully and a spur. Then there is a slow, gradual descent over Uillt na Teanga to the forest track. You could make a detour to see the waterfalls.

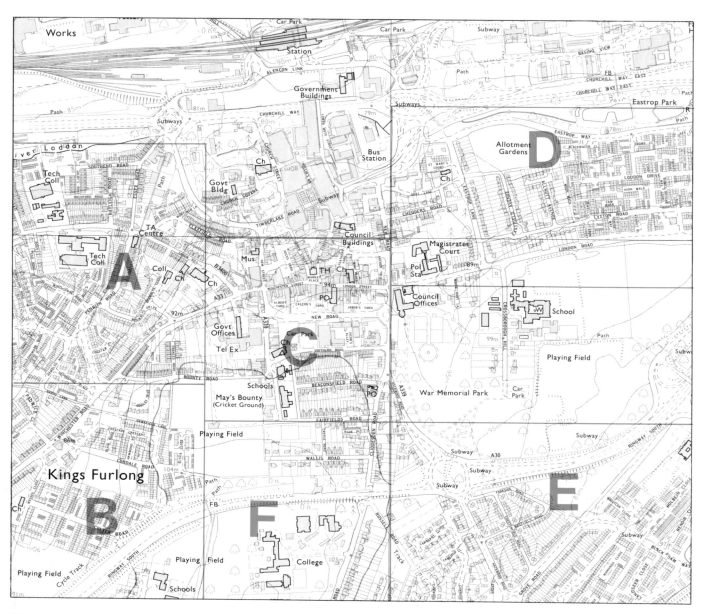

Map 52

One of the most important decisions many of us make is choosing where to live. Although some people (those living in homes allocated by the council, for example) can't choose their own homes, a great many buy or rent houses or flats that they themselves have carefully selected. Naturally, we don't always find the ideal house, for there are the obvious problems of price and availability, and the need to live near where we work.

What is important to us when we select a home is to choose first of all the right town, then the right

neighbourhood, then the right street and finally the right house.

An Ordnance Survey 1:10 000 scale map (for example, Map 52, above) enables us to see which neighbourhood would be appropriate. We can then focus on the right street with a 1:2500 plan (Map 53, page 80). To see the plots of individual houses really clearly, we can use a 1:1250 plan (Map 54, page 82).

Look at Maps 52, 53 and 54. They all relate to the town of Basingstoke in Hampshire.

Information that large-scale OS maps can give about a neighbourhood includes:

1. **The density of the housing**
   We can see how close together the houses are, and the size of the gardens.
2. **Street layouts**
   We can get a good idea of what the environment is like by looking at the street names and patterns (see pages 28 to 30).

3. **Accessibility**
   The maps will show how far it is to the shopping centre, library, park, school, ring road, industrial estate and so on.

What this kind of map cannot show is the likely *ownership* of the houses. We cannot usually tell whether the houses are privately owned or rented out by landlords, housing associations or the local authority.

Neighbourhood		Scores (poor = 1, reasonable = 2, good = 3)										
	Location	Nearness to town centre	Nearness to local shops	Nearness to schools	Nearness to open spaces	Nearness to main roads	Nearness to rail station	Nearness to a church	General housing density	Any other factors you think important	Total score (maximum 30 points)	Rank (first to sixth)
A	Near Technical College											
B	Kings Furlong											
C	New Road area											
D	North of London Road											
E	South of the Ringway											
F	Wallis Road area											

Fig. 70   *Quality of location index*

Exercise 52

Imagine you are moving to Basingstoke. You have decided to buy a house just south of the town centre (see Map 52). To help you select the most suitable part of this area, a quality of location index can be devised. It sounds complex, but is really quite simple.

The chart (Fig. 70) lists six different neighbourhoods (A to F on the map) and a series of headings, such as 'nearness to town centre'.

1. *Copy the chart and award each neighbourhood points under the headings (one point for 'poor', two for 'reasonable', three for 'good').*
2. *Add up the scores for each of the six neighbourhoods and*

place them in order, from best to worst.
3. *Write a description of the environmental quality of the two neighbourhoods you have classed as best and worst.*
4. *Not everyone will agree with your choices. Which area do you think the following people would rate as best?*
   (a) *A student who wants to live within five minutes' walk of both the technical college and the town centre*
   (b) *A retired person looking for a small house near an allotment garden*
   (c) *A teacher who would like a detached house with a large garden, away from the town centre and near open land*

Assume that you choose neighbourhood C in the 'quality of location index' exercise on page 79. Beaconsfield Road seems to fit the bill, because the houses have sizeable gardens and are near the shopping centre, a church, two schools, a cricket ground and the War Memorial Park. Now we need to examine the Beaconsfield Road environment more closely, using a 1:2500 scale plan (Map 53).

Map 53

At the scale of 1:2500, 1 mm on the map represents 2.5 metres on the ground. So it would be possible, for instance, to measure the size of the garden of 13 Beaconsfield Road to the nearest metre. The OS have an equivalent map for your street. You can usually see one in a library or in council offices.

Exercise 53

1. *Look at Map 53. Judging from the information provided, and assuming that you have a free choice, which house would you most like to live in?*
2. *What amenities are provided for residents of this neighbourhood?*
3. *What possible sources of noise or unpleasant views can you detect on this map?*
4. *Which road would appear to have the most traffic using it? How might this affect house prices?*
5. *What is your overall impression of the environmental quality of this neighbourhood?*

Photo 47   *Jubilee Road, Basingstoke*

Exercise 54

Assume that you are married and could afford the mortgage and the down payment on a £30 000 house without too much hardship, a £40 000 house if you sacrifice your holidays, motoring and some leisure activities, and a £50 000 house only if you make a very special effort and if both of you work full time. After reading these estate agents' advertisements for houses in the Beaconsfield Road area of Basingstoke which house might you select?

Jubilee Road
A special opportunity to purchase this favourably situated compact terraced house in a much sought after location near to the church. Convenient for town centre, schools and amenities. Sitting-room, dining/kitchen area, scullery, 2 bedrooms, box-room, bathroom. Compact, easily maintained patio garden at rear. Free car-parking in street opposite after 6 p.m. and on Sundays. Gas fire in sitting-room. Roof recently renovated, with 2 years' guarantee remaining. In a reasonable state of repair, but would benefit from redeco-ration. A fine prospect for a young couple with an interest in D.I.Y. Leasehold.
Rateable value £125
Offered for sale at £24 950

Southern Road
A unique opportunity to acquire this immaculately presented turn-of-the-century mid-terrace house. Features include 3 bedrooms, 2 reception rooms, kitchen, bathroom and a garden at rear with a lawn and flower borders. There is access to the loft, which has a roof light. Double glazing. Electric night storage-heaters. Low-level W.C. Garden shed. Freehold. The condition of the house must be seen to be appreciated.
Rateable value £202
Offered at £32 850

Beaconsfield Road
This house will appeal to those who want plenty of garden space, and who have been waiting for the rare chance to obtain a house in this much sought after road. Although the surroundings are pleasant, with well established residences, the town centre is just a short walk away. Features include a 27-foot lounge, extra dining-room, fitted kitchen, 3 bedrooms, gas central heating, south-facing garden, garage at the rear of the property reached by a private service road. Freehold.
Rateable value £219
Offered at £41 995

Fairfields Road
This excellent Edwardian property will appeal to those seeking a family home with space and character. The present owners have carried out improvements with a delightful end result. Entrance hall, 3 reception rooms, 4 spacious bedrooms, fitted kitchen/breakfast room, family bathroom, gas central heating. Gardens to front and rear. The latter is fully enclosed and magnifi-cently stocked with mature shrubs and trees. Freehold.
Rateable value £265
Offered at £52 750

Note: Although we are using Map 53 for a role-play exercise, the area shown is of course a real place. It has therefore been necessary to alter some of the details of the estate agents' material and to invent other details in order to protect the residents' privacy.

Map 54

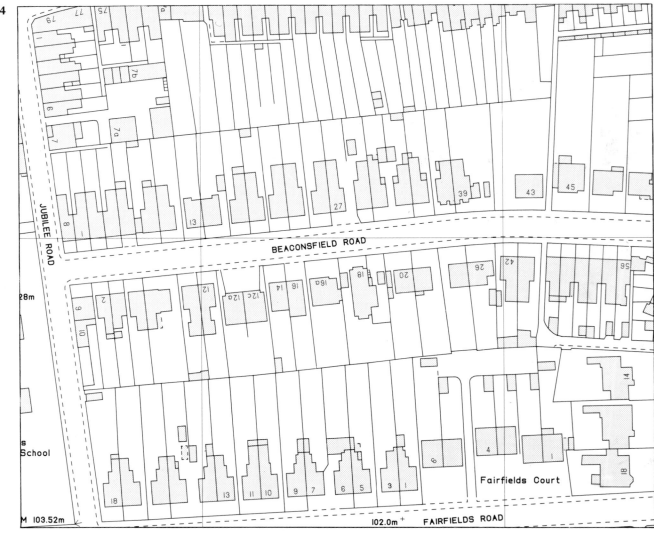

This map is drawn to a scale of 1:1250 and is the largest-scale plan published by the OS. It shows Beaconsfield Road in great detail. To appreciate just how detailed this map is, turn back to Maps 53, 52, 40, 42 and 47 (keep to that order).

Exercise 55

These questions help to emphasize the level of information that 1:1250 plans of a street offer.

1. *Where would you park your car if you lived in*
   - *(a) 4 Fairfields Court?*
   - *(b) 18 Fairfields Road?*
   - *(c) 39 Beaconsfield Road?*
   - *(d) 3 Beaconsfield Road?*
   - *(e) 29 Beaconsfield Road?*
2. *Which house has the largest garden?*
3. *What do you think caused the unusual layout of 7, 7a, and 7b Jubilee Road?*
4. *(a) Which houses look the most modern in layout?*
   - *(b) When do you think most of the houses in Beaconsfield Road were built?*
5. *What do you think the outbuildings at the end of some of the gardens are?*

Photo 48 *Fairfields Road, Basingstoke*

Detailed, large-scale maps are of interest to farmers as well as town-dwellers. These maps pinpoint individual farm buildings, give the exact position of fences and hedges and show the area of each field.

Map 55 (below) shows a farm, Salter Street Farm in Warwickshire, drawn to a scale of 1:2500. This extract covers only part of a 1-kilometre grid square. The actual size of the area, on the ground, is only 300 metres by 475 metres, so the foot-bridge crossing the moat is five metres long.

Maps drawn to the scale of 1:2500 are ideal for conducting **land-use surveys**. The generally accepted classification and coding for land-use mapping is as follows:

Arable land (used for growing crops): brown
Market gardening (flowers and vegetables): purple
Orchards (commercial growing of fruit trees): purple/ white stripes
Grassland (for grazing animals): light green
Woodland: dark green
Heath, moorland and rough land: yellow
Open space (parks, playing-fields, etc.): lime green
Water: blue

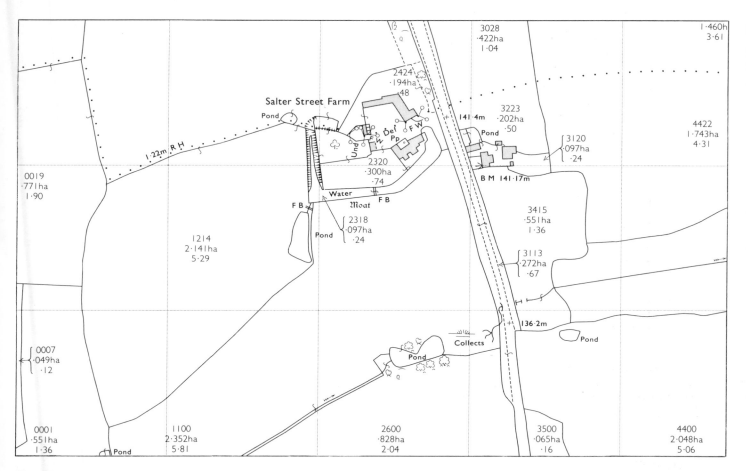

Map 55

Exercise 56

1. *What suggests that Salter Street Farm is on a site of historic interest?*

2. *Draw a sketch-map of the farm buildings. Label each one to show how you think it is used.*

3. *You will notice that the fields are labelled with numbers as well as their size in hectares and acres. Make a land-use map of the farm. Begin by tracing the field boundaries. Then, using the shading suggested above, colour in the fields.*

Land use
Fields 1100, 1214, 4422: arable   Field 3028: orchard
Field 2424: woodland   Field 2320: open space
Fields 3415, 3120: market crops   Field 3113: rough land

4. *Match the following field numbers with the correct descriptions:*

1100

2424

3223

3500

(a) *A field with some badly drained land in one corner*
(b) *A field that has been amalgamated with another to make it easier to cultivate*
(c) *A field where a shelter belt has been planted*
(d) *A field too small to use machinery in very effectively*

5. *If you were the farmer and had decided to turn one field into a caravan and camping site, which would you choose? Give your reasons.*

Photo 49   *An urban motorway under construction*

Planning blight occurs when rumours spread around that a major new development is likely to take place in a particular area within the next few years. The new development could be an urban motorway, a new shopping complex, a new factory or perhaps a power-station. Its construction will probably involve demolishing some houses and lower the value of others. As a result of this threat, house prices fall and people who want to move away cannot find anybody willing to buy their homes.

Note: Exercise 57 is not based on any known planning proposals. It relates purely imaginary plans to a real map to test people's values and attitudes.

Exercise 57

The photograph of Wigan on page 72 shows how easily a main road in a town can become blocked by heavy traffic. One solution is to construct an urban motorway, but that can cause a massive disruption to the life of a neighbourhood.

As a simulation exercise, let us imagine that proposals have been made for an urban motorway to link the centre of Barnsley with Junction 37 of the M1 motorway.

1. *Suggest a route for this motorway link that might cause the minimum damage to residential areas, and to the commercial life of the town centre.*
2. *Suggest which areas might suffer most from planning blight.*
3. *If you were a resident of one of these areas, how might you oppose the urban-motorway plans?*
4. *Suggest other instances (not just around Barnsley) where planning blight could occur.*

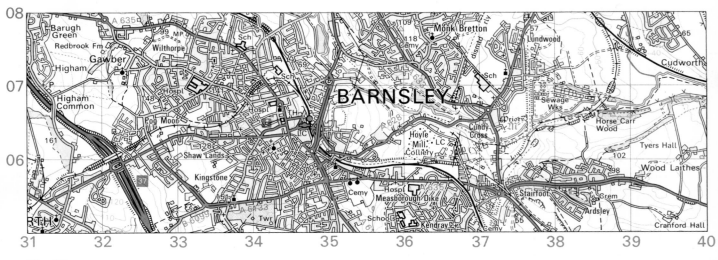

Map 56

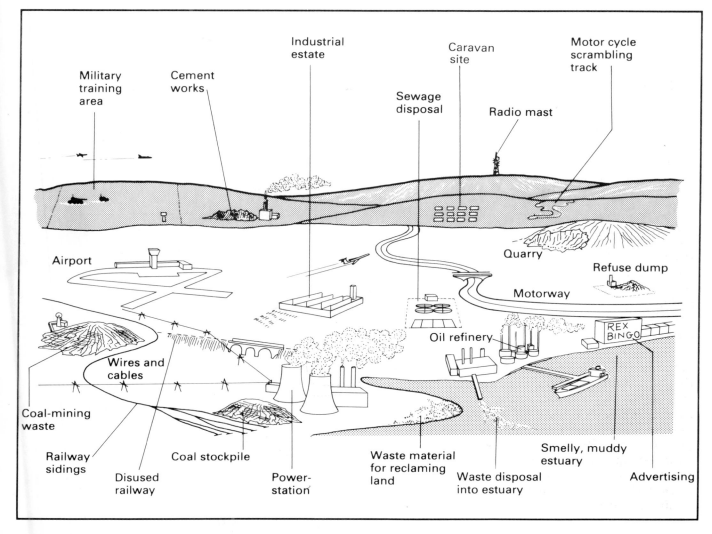

Military training area — Cement works — Industrial estate — Caravan site — Motor cycle scrambling track — Sewage disposal — Radio mast — Airport — Quarry — Refuse dump — Motorway — Oil refinery — REX BINGO — Wires and cables — Coal-mining waste — Railway sidings — Disused railway — Coal stockpile — Power-station — Waste material for reclaming land — Waste disposal into estuary — Smelly, muddy estuary — Advertising

Fig. 71   *Possible sources of pollution*

Owing to modern industrial and scientific progress and the noisy ways in which many people enjoy their leisure, our environment is constantly under threat. The word 'pollution' is used to describe various types of environmental damage. Pollution comes in four main forms:

1. *Air pollution*, which can create smoke, dust, grit, toxic gases and acid rain.
2. *Water pollution*, where toxic waste products, sewage, oil and hot water can be dumped into rivers, lakes, estuaries or the sea.
3. *Noise pollution* from factories, quarries, traffic, airports, leisure activities, etc.
4. *Visual pollution* from ugly derelict land, mining waste, electricity pylons, wires, litter, etc.

Many of the developments since the Industrial Revolution have entailed environmental changes that cannot be reversed. Developments that involve large-scale earth-moving are bound to make changes as profound as the effects of rivers and glaciers. Once an industry has finished with a site, it is often reluctant to spend large sums of money tidying it up. So it seems likely that the earth's inhabitants in the year 4000 may still see signs of our railways, quarries, reservoirs, docks, motorways and airports.

For most people, pollution poses a problem. We want electricity but not power-stations, air travel without airports, petrol without oil refineries. We need products. We need jobs. We need places to enjoy ourselves. We also want to keep our environment as pleasant and as natural as possible.

Exercise 58
1. *Look at the diagram of the polluted landscape. Place each of the sources of pollution in one of the four categories listed above.*
2. *Choose one example of pollution from each category. How could that type of pollution be reduced or even eliminated altogether?*

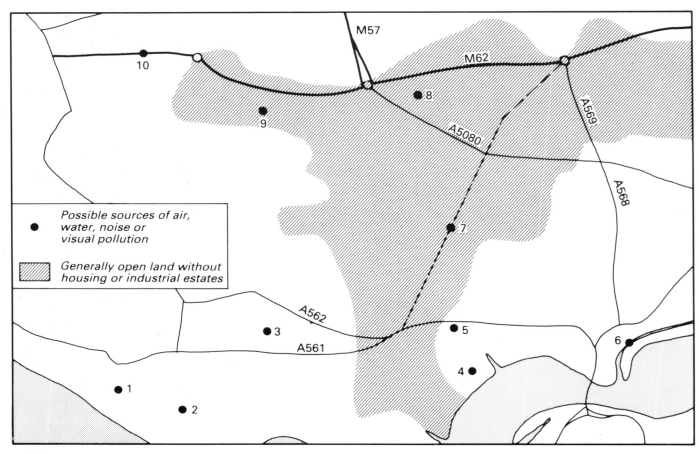

Fig. 72 *Sketch-map of the area between Liverpool and Widnes*

Exercise 59

Fig. 72 is based on Map 57, which shows the area between Liverpool and Widnes. Like many industrial zones, this area is inevitably subject to some forms of pollution, even though great efforts have been made in recent years towards conservation and control.

1. *List the ten possible sources of pollution shown in Fig. 72 (they may include ugly views and unpleasant smells as well as noise, smoke and waste-dumping). Use Map 57.*
2. *If you were a town planner charged with the task of improving the environment, which five of the items marked 1 to 10 on the sketch-map would you tackle first?*
3. *The open space shaded in on the sketch-map (Fig. 72) lies on the boundary of a big city. How might that land be under threat from residents of that city?*
4. *Merseyside is an area of high unemployment. Should a large, and perhaps ugly, new factory be constructed on open ground, say in grid square 4685? Are jobs more or less important than the environment? What type of compromise, if any, should be made?*

Note: Levels of pollution are no worse in Liverpool than in many other industrial cities. Indeed, great efforts have been made to improve the landscape of Liverpool. This map extract was used because it shows a variety of industrial and residential developments in a compact location. Sadly, the edge of any large city will show comparable pollution and environmental problems.

Photo 50 *Urban fringe pollution*

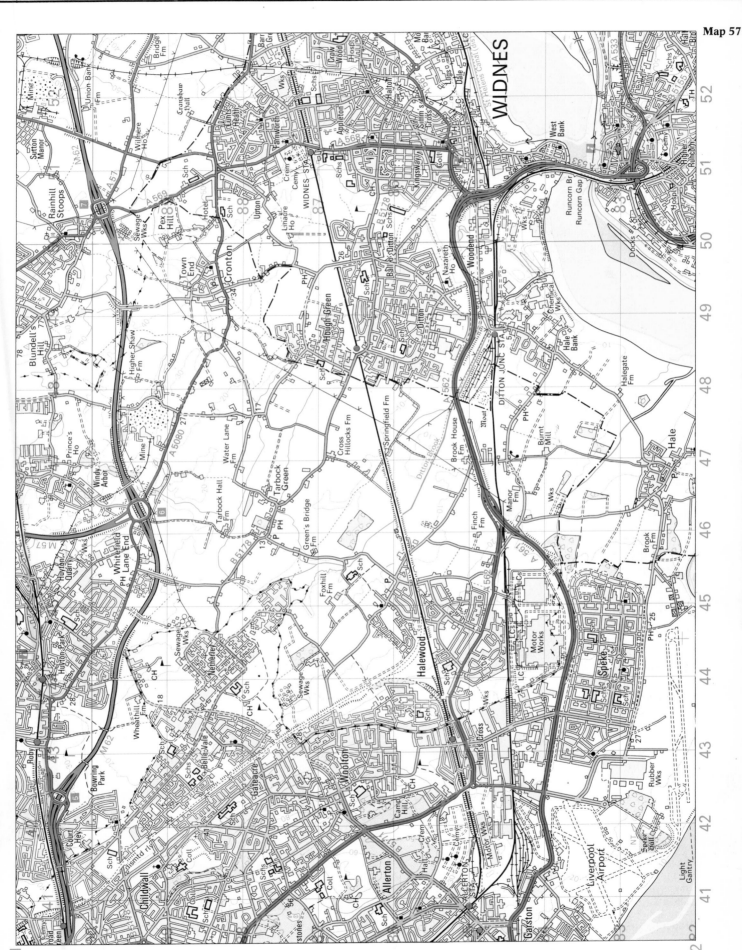

CHANGES IN THE LOCAL AREA

Anyone who leaves an area and returns to it some years later is usually surprised by the number of changes they notice. New buildings may have gone up and old ones come down. New roads may have been built, old railway lines and canals shut down. It is often hard to remember what a place was like in the past. Old photographs help a great deal, but historic OS maps give a *total* picture of a place as surveyed in a given year.

Maps 58 to 61 are four map extracts, drawn to scales of 1:10 560 and 1:10 000, of the mill village of Higham in Lancashire. They are dated 1847, 1895, 1938 and 1980.

Before you look more closely at these four maps, think about the many changes taking place in your local area. Can you list examples of any of the following, or similar changes?

- New houses being built on fields
- Old terraced houses being demolished
- The closure of old churches, cinemas, theatres, railway stations, etc.
- The opening of new out-of-town shopping centres
- The building of a bypass or ring road
- The extension of an airport runway and terminal
- The closing of an old mill
- The closing of a village school
- The opening of a country park

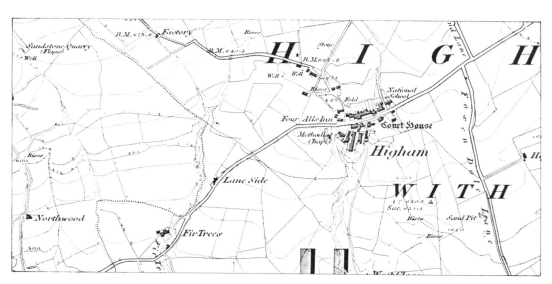

Map 58   *1847*

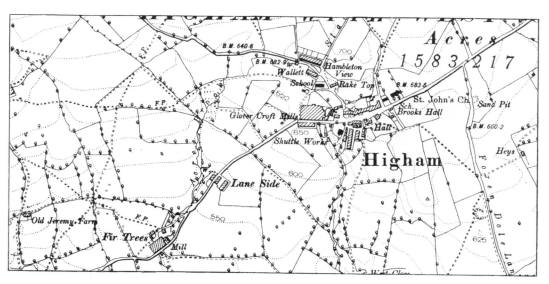

Map 59   *1895*

Exercise 60

Use the four maps of Higham to help you answer these questions.

1. *Describe the features of Higham shown on the 1847 map.*
2. *What changes were brought about by industry by 1895?*
3. *What further changes had occurred by 1938?*
4. *What sort of settlement is Higham today?*
5. *How did field boundaries change between 1847 and 1980?*
6. *What changes occurred in the road system, and when?*
7. *Comment on the provision of footpaths on each map.*
8. *Trace the history of the development of schools in Higham.*
9. *Imagine an OS map of Higham printed in 2010. How might it differ from the 1980 map? Draw a map showing Higham in 2010, with all the changes you think likely.*

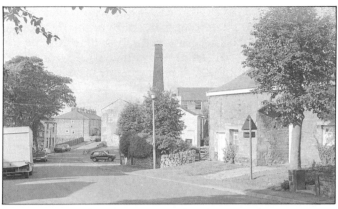

Photo 51 *The historic centre of Higham village. The mill chimney belongs to Clover Croft Mill, built in 1852. Were was the picture taken from? What other buildings can you identify?*

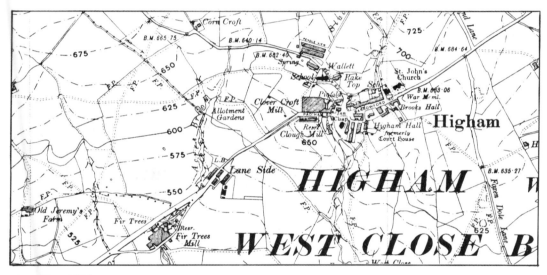

Map 60 *1938*

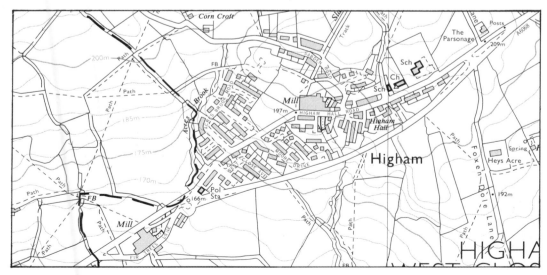

Map 61 *1980*

We have just seen how old OS maps can give us 'snapshots' of a landscape or settlement in a particular year in the past. Modern OS maps show us the relics of the past that are still visible today. A 1:50 000 or 1:25 000 OS map contains a surprising amount of historical information. Careful detective work, using the clues provided by the map-makers, can help us build up a fascinating picture of Britain in past centuries.

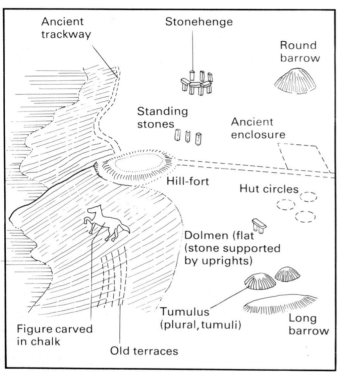

Fig. 73 *Prehistoric features*

Prehistoric Remains

This drawing shows some of the common prehistoric remains that are indicated on OS maps (see the maps on pages 39, 43, 48 and 54). Many of these remains, such as *barrows*, *tumuli* and *dolmens*, show how people of the Stone Age, Bronze Age or Iron Age were buried. Others show how they lived *(hut circles)*, how they defended themselves *(hill-forts)*, how they travelled *(ancient bridle-ways)* and possibly how they worshipped *(stone circles* and *standing stones)*.

Most of these prehistoric remains are found on open downland and moorland away from areas that were once heavily forested.

Exercise 61

1. *How many of the features shown in Fig. 73 can you find on the Quantock Hills of Somerset (Map 34, page 43)? List them with their grid references.*
2. *What additional prehistoric features not shown on the diagram appear on the Dartmoor map (page 39)?*

Photo 52 *Hadrian's Wall, Housesteads, Northumberland, built by the Romans in A.D. 122*

Roman Remains

The Romans were the first people to build towns in Britain, and many places whose names end in 'chester', 'cester' or 'caster' are of Roman origin. Look for such remains as a *villa*, a *Roman road*, a *fort* or a *milecastle*.

Exercise 62

1. *Name some towns and cities that you think may have been of Roman origin.*
2. *Using the map extracts in this book (Map 37, page 48, for example), hunt for evidence of Roman occupation. Note the symbol for Roman antiquities shown on page 4.*

Medieval Remains

Medieval towns had many churches and public buildings crammed between winding, narrow streets and hemmed in by protective walls. There would probably have been a large *castle*. In the countryside can be seen *manor-houses*, medieval village layouts, ancient field boundaries, old hunting forests, and the sites of battles. Durham (Map 40) shows many of the features of a medieval town centre. Several clear examples of villages of medieval origin attached to *halls* and *manors* can be seen in Norfolk (Maps 18, 19).

Exercise 63
Match the following medieval features with the correct locations:

abbey	Edlesborough (Map 39, page 54)
castle	Trunch (Map 3, page 8)
moat	Buckfast (Map 32, page 39)
tithe barn	Salter Street (Map 55, page 83)
manor-house	Peveril (Map 30, page 35)

Photo 53 *Harlech Castle, Wales, dates from the thirteenth century.*

Industrial Archaeology

The enormous expansion in industry that came with the introduction of steam-power in the nineteenth century has left its mark very clearly on most British towns. It is usually easy to detect an old *canal*, a *disused railway*, a derelict *mill*, an abandoned *tunnel* or an old *mine*. The study of these old industrial remains and attempts to imagine what the landscape was like when all these features were in full operation are called *industrial archaeology*.

Exercise 64
The Don Valley of Sheffield (Map 29) developed as a coal-mining, steel-making and cutlery manufacturing zone. List the notable features of nineteenth-century development shown on Map 29 (page 32).

Photo 54 *Once the major carriers of bulk traffic in Britain, canals are now little used except for recreation.*

Modern History

There have been more rapid changes in this century than in any other. Not only have two world wars taken place, but motor vehicles and aircraft have been become commonplace; social changes have created and then destroyed things like cinemas and theatres. Some twentieth-century features you can see on maps, like old airfields and disused railway lines, already look like relics of the past.

Exercise 65
The Second World War made significant changes to the landscape in a very short time. Most notable perhaps are the many airfields that are now disused; also, many coastlines show signs of old wartime defences.
Using Maps 19 (page 23), 39 (page 54) and 41 (page 61), list some of the changes that twentieth-century historians would be interested in recording.

Photo 55 *This abandoned control tower is all that remains of London's first international airport at Croydon.*

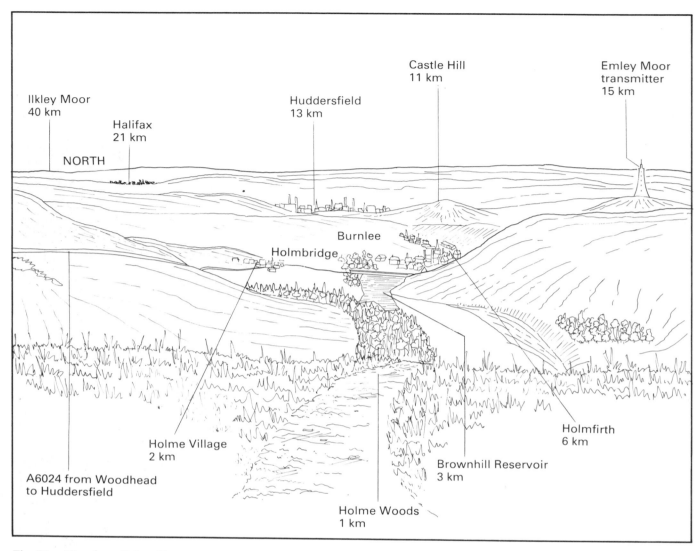

Fig. 74   *View from Holme Moss*

Exercise 66

It's nice to end this book by enjoying a good view with the help of an OS map, a photograph and a field sketch. They all show part of the Pennines from the Holmfirth area. When you look at such a view, what you want to know is exactly what you can see. Try to identify the features in the drawing by matching them with the map and the photograph, which was taken near the Holme Moss television station (095040).

1. *In what compass direction was the camera pointing?*
2. *Give the grid references of the following:*
   (a) Brownhill Reservoir
   (b) Holmfirth church tower
   (c) Holme village
   (d) Holmbridge church tower
3. *(a) How far is it by road from the Holme Moss television station to Holmfirth church?*
   (b) Give four reasons why travel along the A6024 might be slow.

Map-reading is not only a most valuable skill to possess, but a key to the greater enjoyment and appreciation of landscapes both in towns and in the countryside. In some situations good map-reading can save time and money. In extreme cases it could save life.

'OK, I can do the navigating. I know where to go.'

Photo 56 *The view from Holme Moss, looking towards Holmfirth*

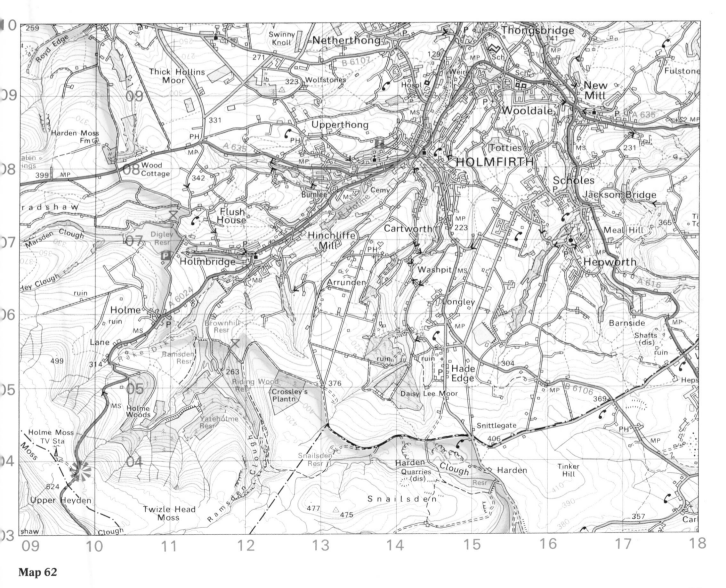

Map 62

CONCEPTS AND SKILLS COVERED IN THIS BOOK

ORDNANCE SURVEY MAPS USED IN THIS BOOK

The maps used in this book are extracts from the Ordnance Survey maps listed below.
The largest scale map used is 1:1250. The smallest scale map used is 1:1 375 000.

Scale	OS Sheet Number	OS Sheet Name	Map Number
1:1250	SU 6351 NE		54
1:2500	SP 1274/1374		55
1:2500	SU 6251/6351		53
1:10 000	SD 83 NW		61
1:10 000	SU 65 SW		52
1:10 000	NY 76 NE		20
1:10 000	SE 65 SE		21
1:10 000	ST 76 NW		22
1:10 000		Town Map: Doncaster	23, 24, 25, 26, 27, 28
1:10 560	SD 83 NW		58, 59, 60
Pathfinder Maps			
1:25 000	SO 49/59	Church Stretton	37
1:25 000	SP 81/91	Aylesbury and Tring	39
1:25 000	NZ 24/34	Durham	40
Landranger Maps			
1:50 000	32	South Skye	38,51
1:50 000	59	St Andrews and Kirkcaldy	16, 35, 41
1:50 000	88	Tyneside and Durham	45
1:50 000	108	Liverpool	46, 48, 57
1:50 000	110	Sheffield and Huddersfield	29, 30, 33, 56, 62
1:50 000	133	North East Norfolk	3, 18, 19
1:50 000	181	Minehead and Brendon Hills	6, 34
1:50 000	182	Weston-super-Mare & Bridgwater	4, 5, 7, 8, 9, 10, 11, 12, 13, 17, 50
1:50 000	196	Solent and the Isle of Wight	2, 14, 15, 36
Tourist Map			
1:63 360	—	Tourist Map: Dartmoor	31, 32
Routemaster Maps			
1:250 000	7	Wales and the West Midlands	44
1:250 000	9	South East England	1, 49
Routeplanner Map			
1:625 000	—	Routeplanner Map	42
Planning Map			
1:1 375 000	—	This extract is taken from the *Ordnance Survey Motoring Atlas*.	47

Arnold-Wheaton
A Division of E. J. Arnold & Son Limited
Parkside Lane, Leeds LS11 5TD

A member of the Pergamon Group
Headington Hill Hall, Oxford OX3 0BW

First published 1985 by Arnold-Wheaton, Parkside Lane, Dewsbury Road, Leeds and Ordnance Survey, Romsey Road, Maybush, Southampton
Second Impression 1986
Third Impression 1988

Printed in Great Britain by A. Wheaton & Co. Ltd, Hennock Road, Exeter

ISBN 0 560-66710-8

1:25 000 Pathfinder Series Map (Metric)
CONVENTIONAL SIGNS

Ordnance Survey

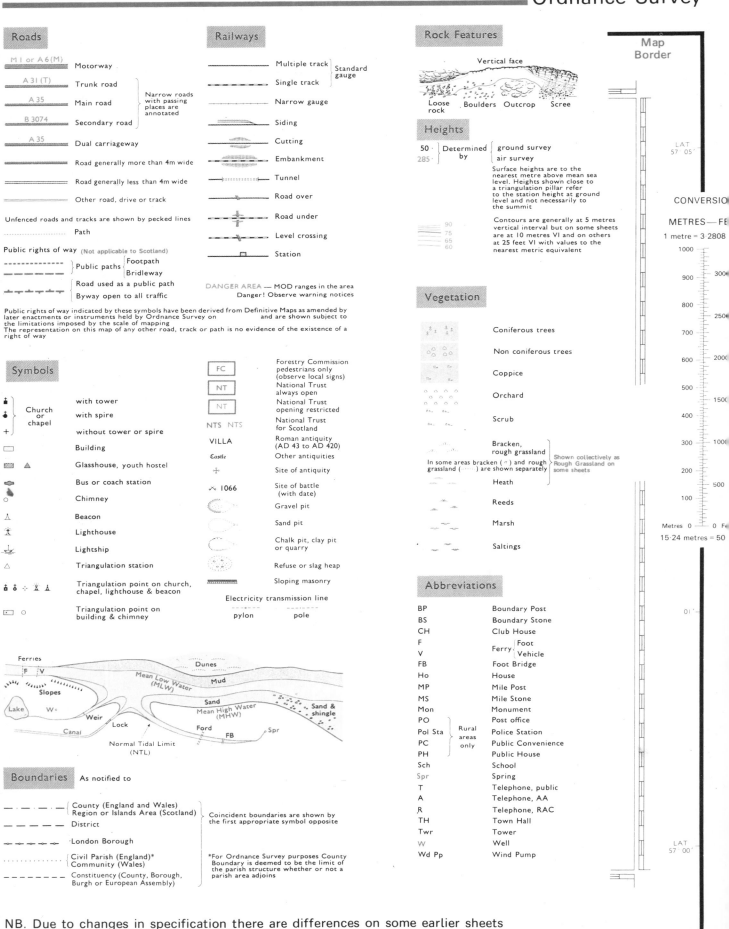

Roads

M 1 or A 6(M)	Motorway
A 31 (T)	Trunk road
A 35	Main road
B 3074	Secondary road
A 35	Dual carriageway
	Road generally more than 4m wide
	Road generally less than 4m wide
	Other road, drive or track

Narrow roads with passing places are annotated

Unfenced roads and tracks are shown by pecked lines

Path

Public rights of way (Not applicable to Scotland)

Public paths { Footpath / Bridleway }

Road used as a public path

Byway open to all traffic

Public rights of way indicated by these symbols have been derived from Definitive Maps as amended by later enactments or instruments held by Ordnance Survey on   and are shown subject to the limitations imposed by the scale of mapping
The representation on this map of any other road, track or path is no evidence of the existence of a right of way

Symbols

Church or chapel	with tower / with spire / without tower or spire
	Building
	Glasshouse, youth hostel
	Bus or coach station
	Chimney
	Beacon
	Lighthouse
	Lightship
△	Triangulation station
	Triangulation point on church, chapel, lighthouse & beacon
	Triangulation point on building & chimney

FC	Forestry Commission pedestrians only (observe local signs)
NT	National Trust always open
NT	National Trust opening restricted
NTS NTS	National Trust for Scotland
VILLA	Roman antiquity (AD 43 to AD 420)
Castle	Other antiquities
	Site of antiquity
⚔ 1066	Site of battle (with date)
	Gravel pit
	Sand pit
	Chalk pit, clay pit or quarry
	Refuse or slag heap
	Sloping masonry

Electricity transmission line
pylon   pole

Railways

	Multiple track } Standard gauge
	Single track }
	Narrow gauge
	Siding
	Cutting
	Embankment
	Tunnel
	Road over
	Road under
	Level crossing
	Station

DANGER AREA — MOD ranges in the area
Danger! Observe warning notices

Rock Features

Vertical face

Loose rock   Boulders   Outcrop   Scree

Heights

50 ·	Determined by	ground survey
285 ·		air survey

Surface heights are to the nearest metre above mean sea level. Heights shown close to a triangulation pillar refer to the station height at ground level and not necessarily to the summit

90 / 75 / 65 / 60	Contours are generally at 5 metres vertical interval but on some sheets are at 10 metres VI and on others at 25 feet VI with values to the nearest metric equivalent

Vegetation

	Coniferous trees
	Non coniferous trees
	Coppice
	Orchard
	Scrub
	Bracken, rough grassland
	Heath
	Reeds
	Marsh
	Saltings

In some areas bracken ( ) and rough grassland ( ) are shown separately
Shown collectively as Rough Grassland on some sheets

Abbreviations

BP	Boundary Post
BS	Boundary Stone
CH	Club House
F	Ferry { Foot
V	Vehicle }
FB	Foot Bridge
Ho	House
MP	Mile Post
MS	Mile Stone
Mon	Monument
PO	Post office
Pol Sta	Police Station } Rural areas only
PC	Public Convenience
PH	Public House
Sch	School
Spr	Spring
T	Telephone, public
A	Telephone, AA
R	Telephone, RAC
TH	Town Hall
Twr	Tower
W	Well
Wd Pp	Wind Pump

Ferries

Dunes
Mean Low Water (MLW)
Mud
Slopes
Lake   W
Sand
Mean High Water (MHW)
Sand & shingle
Weir
Lock
Canal
Ford
FB
Spr
Normal Tidal Limit (NTL)

Map Border

LAT 57° 05'

CONVERSIO

METRES — FE

1 metre = 3·2808

Metres	Feet
1000	
900	300
800	250
700	200
600	
500	150
400	
300	100
200	
100	50
Metres 0	0 F

15·24 metres = 50

01'

LAT 57° 00'

Boundaries   As notified to

	County (England and Wales) / Region or Islands Area (Scotland)
	District
	London Borough
	Civil Parish (England)* / Community (Wales)
	Constituency (County, Borough, Burgh or European Assembly)

Coincident boundaries are shown by the first appropriate symbol opposite

*For Ordnance Survey purposes County Boundary is deemed to be the limit of the parish structure whether or not a parish area adjoins

NB. Due to changes in specification there are differences on some earlier sheets

Made and published by the Director General of the Ordnance Survey, Southampton